To Preach or Not to Preach

Women's Ministry Then and Now

William Varner

Phil 4:2-3

DEDICATION

This book is affectionately dedicated to:

HELEN

who

"looks well to the ways of her household,"

so that

"her children rise up and bless her"

and

"her husband also, and he praises her."

(Proverbs 31:27-28)

CONTENTS

PREFACE

This book about the ministry of women in the New Testament church is a revised, updated, and expanded edition of a thesis presented in 1976 for the Master in Theology (NT) degree at Biblical Theological Seminary in Hatfield, PA. I have attempted to examine all the Biblical texts that relate to the ministry of women in the New Testament period. I write from the perspective of what has been called complementarianism. Although much has been written about the ministry of women since 1976, the arguments that support the right of women to be ordained as elders and overseers have not really changed that much! I have sought, however, to interact with some of the recent literature that offers nuanced reasons for women sharing the same level of ministry as men in the New Testament period. I have tried to take notice of the most articulate authors who offer these "new" arguments. I have also added a bibliography of books and articles that have appeared since 1976 which have addressed both the complementarian and egalitarian views of women's ministry. This bibliography, totaling 250 articles and monographs before and after 1976, may offer the greatest help to someone who desires to research this subject further.

Dr. Gary Cohen – professor, parishioner, and friend – served as my advisor during my post-graduate work and was a constant encouragement through his gracious assistance and advice. The library staffs at Biblical and Westminster Seminaries and The Master's University and Seminary were very helpful during the research, writing, and expansion of the work. The brothers and sisters in the Sojourners Fellowship at Grace Community Church have been tremendously supportive in praying for their pastor. Thanks also to my wife, Helen, who retyped the entire thesis from a rather crude PDF provided by the library at Columbia International University when it was discovered that the thesis was missing from the

Biblical Seminary library!

My research assistant while he was a student at The Master's Seminary, Peter Goeman, also helped in preparing the manuscript for publication. Thanks also to a member of my Nerdy Language Majors Facebook group, Daniel Buck, for his suggestions. My deep appreciation is also extended to Dr. John MacArthur for contributing the Foreword and for never being hesitant to take unpopular positions which he believes are supported by the Word of God.

Scripture quotations are from the New American Standard Bible (1995) or from the author's own translation.

FOREWORD

It is clear from the biblical record that the early church was led by men from the beginning. All the apostles were men. Elders in the church were men and did the teaching whenever the church came together. Every text dealing with the issue in the Pauline epistles is unequivocal about male leadership. In fact, Paul's statements against women teaching men are so emphatic that some have wrongly accused the apostle of being a misogynist.

Dr. William Varner has written this wonderful analytical compendium of every significant Scripture pertaining to gender roles in public worship. Rather than cherry-picking the texts that can be easily spun to support one side or the other, he considers everything Scripture has to say about the subject. Most helpfully, he begins in the first chapter with a careful, insightful overview of Old Testament worship. He highlights the role of women in relationship to Temple worship, public praise, and the priesthood. He demonstrates that alongside the obvious patriarchal quality of Old Testament religion, women were by no means excluded or even marginalized. The roles of men and women were different, to be sure, but women were highly and consistently honored, not repressed or degraded, throughout Old Testament history. Ministry opportunities for women were abundant.

The same principle holds true in the New Testament. Men and women are called to different roles and given different responsibilities in the church. "Different" does not mean lesser, greater, more or less responsible, or otherwise inequitable. Men and women are equal in dignity, and Scripture plainly says that both genders stand together on equal ground before God in Christ—we are all one in Him (Galatians 3:28).

The truth that God has appointed us to different roles is obvious in many ways. It is perhaps most plainly seen in procreation, parenting, and the partnership of marriage. Men and women *naturally* fulfill different roles. We were made differently for our respective purposes. And it was God Himself who designed us that way. Christians do not have to buy the worldly lie that gender differences are somehow inherently unfair and repressive.

The best feature of this book is the succinct way Dr. Varner has brought together all the biblical data in a meticulous, methodical, clear, and persuasive study—all neatly framed in a simple, easily accessible format. The value of this volume is far out of proportion to its compact size. It is the most helpful and reader-friendly resource I've seen on the subject to date.

— John MacArthur

WHAT WAS IT LIKE BACK THEN?

To better understand the New Testament teaching about the ministry of women, it is necessary to survey the public religious role of women in the Old Testament and also during the "Second Temple" period prior to the first century AD. Therefore, let us begin to enter a very Jewish world.

Woman's Religious Role in the Old Testament

Woman's religious role in the Old Testament could be described as one of *limited participation*. The first obvious fact of her role is that there was no order of "priestesses" provided for in the Mosaic legislation. Priests were "the sons of Aaron," namely, Nadab, Abihu, Eleazar, and Ithamar, and their male descendants (Exo 28:1; Num 18:1-7). However, this exclusion of women from the priesthood did not mean her exclusion from the religious service of the tabernacle and temple. Both men and women contributed their gold jewelry to help construct the tabernacle (Exo 35:22). Bezaleel made the laver of bronze from one of these contributions from women. "Moreover, he made the laver of bronze with its base of bronze, from the mirrors of the serving women who served at the doorway of the tent of meeting" (Exo 38:8). It is never stated clearly what the exact work of these "serving women" entailed. However, in later years they became involved illicitly with unprincipled priests. "Now Eli was very old; and he heard all that his sons were doing to all Israel, and how they lay with the women who served at the doorway of the tent of meeting" (1 Sam 2:22).

There seems to be evidence that both men and women could offer sacrifices since they both had to confess and make restitution.

Speak to the sons of Israel, 'When a man or

woman commits any of the sins of mankind, acting unfaithfully against the LORD, and that person is guilty, then he shall confess his sins which he has committed, and he shall make restitution in full for his wrong, and add to it one-fifth of it, and give it to him whom he has wronged (Num 5:6-7; Lev 12).

Women, along with men, were eligible to take the Nazirite vow. "Speak to the sons of Israel, and say to them, 'When a man or woman makes a special vow, the vow of a Nazarite...'" (Num 6:2). However, if a daughter made a vow to the Lord and her father heard about it and forbade it, "none of her vows or her obligations by which she has bound herself shall stand; and the Lord will forgive her because her father had forbidden her" (Num 30:5). The same was true of a husband's right to annul a wife's vow on the day he heard of it. However, if he said nothing to her on that day, he confirmed her vows and they were binding. In other words, at some later date he could not annul the vow (Num 30:13-15). There were other limitations and exemptions regarding woman's religious role in the Old Testament. Women were exempt from the requirement to attend three feasts at Jerusalem. "Three times a year all your males shall appear before the Lord God" (Exo 23:17; see also Exo 34:23 and Deut 16:16). However, women often accompanied their husbands on such pilgrimages. Hannah accompanied Eli to Shiloh and prayed in the "temple of the Lord" (1 Sam 1:9). An interesting example of her right to exemption from the yearly pilgrimage is in her later refusal to go back to the temple with her husband until the child Samuel was weaned (1 Sam 1:21-22). From this we conclude that the exemption from religious pilgrimage for women was probably due to the domestic hardship that this would often involve. However, sometimes all were to make this pilgrimage.

Then Moses commanded them, saying
"At the end of every seven years, at the

> time of the year of remission of debts,
> at the Feast of Booths, when all Israel
> comes to appear before the Lord your
> God at the place which He will choose,
> you shall read this law in front of all
> Israel in their hearing. "Assemble the
> people, the men and the women and
> children and the alien who is in your
> town, in order that they may hear and
> learn and fear the LORD your God,
> and be careful to observe all the words
> of this law" (Deut 31:10-12).

It is interesting to note that women were accorded the right of hearing the Word on an equal basis with men.

> Then Ezra the priest brought the law
> before the assembly of men, women,
> and all who could listen with
> understanding, on the first day of the
> seventh month. And he read from it
> before the square which was in front of
> the Water Gate from early morning
> until midday, in the presence of men
> and women, those who could
> understand; and all the people were
> attentive to the book of the law (Neh
> 8:2-3).

They evidently were not separated from the men as happened in later synagogue services.

It is also interesting to note that the wife was omitted in the commandment not to work on the Sabbath.

> The seventh day is a sabbath of the
> LORD your God; in it you shall not do

> any work, you or your son or your
> daughter, your male or your female
> servant or your cattle or your sojourner
> who stays with you (Exo 20:10; Deut
> 5:14).

Again the reason seems to be that such abstention from work
would be incompatible with domestic responsibilities. When a
woman gave birth to a child, she was under certain restrictions
regarding her relationship to the sanctuary.

> Speak to the sons of Israel, saying,
> "When a woman gives birth and bears
> a male child, then she shall be unclean
> for seven days, as in the days of her
> menstruation she shall be unclean.
> And on the eighth day the flesh of his
> foreskin shall be circumcised. Then
> she shall remain in the blood of her
> purification for thirty-three days; she
> shall not touch any consecrated thing,
> nor enter the sanctuary, until the days
> of her purification are completed" (Lev
> 12:2-4).

The length of restriction was doubled in the case of a female
child. Although we may wonder what childbirth has to do with
the privilege of public worship, this legislation no doubt served
as a reminder of the hereditary nature of imputed sin.

> Iniquity is imputed to the mother for
> having brought a sinner into the world.
> After the child is circumcised, i.e.,
> recognized as received into covenant
> with Abraham's God, her imputed sin
> is reckoned as in some measure
> removed. But still, though she shares

to some extent in the benefits which her child receives from the covenant of circumcision, she is to touch nothing hallowed, nor come to hallowed ground, for thirty-three days...The child, in after days, must have learnt the lesson of his depravity very deeply, when his mother told him of her forty day's defilement.[1]

It is also evident that women had some sort of musical ministry in Old Testament worship. After the horsemen of Pharaoh were consumed by the waters of the sea, we read:

> And Miriam the prophetess, Aaron's sister, took the tambourines in her hand, and all the women went out after her with tambourines and with dancing. And Miriam answered them, "Sing to the LORD, for He is highly exalted; The horse and his rider He has hurled into the sea" (Exo 15:20-21).

Tambourines were used by women on festive occasions and processions in the temple.

> They have seen Thy procession, O God, The procession of my God, my King, into the sanctuary. The singers went on, the musicians after them, in the midst of the maidens beating tambourines (Psa 68:24-25).

---

[1] Bonar, Andrew. *Exposition of Leviticus* (Grand Rapids: 1970), 99. Bonar's reference to iniquity being imputed to her is debatable.

Before and after the exile, women sang in the temple choirs.

> All these were the sons of Heman the
> king's seer to exalt him according to the
> words of God, for God gave fourteen
> sons and three daughters to Heman.
> All these were under the direction of
> their father to sing in the house of the
> LORD, with cymbals, harps and lyres,
> for the service of the house of God
> (1 Chron 25:5-6).

> The whole assembly together was
> 42,360, besides their male and female
> servants, of whom there were 7,337;
> and they had 245 male and female
> singers (Ezra 2:64-65 and Neh. 7:67).

Although there were no "priestesses" in the Old Testament worship, "prophetesses" appeared in each stage of Israel's history. The first to be called a "prophetess" was Miriam, sister of Moses and Aaron. As has been previously noted, this title is applied to her in Exodus 15:20 as she and the other women sang to the Lord for His hurling the Egyptians into the sea. This is the only example of her "prophesying," although later she claimed that God had spoken through her.

> Then Miriam and Aaron spoke against
> Moses because of the Cushite woman
> whom he had married (for he had married
> a Cushite woman). And they said, "Has the
> LORD indeed spoken only through
> Moses? Has He not spoken through us as
> well?" (Num 12:1-2).

God's indictment against Israel through Micah included the statement that "I sent before you Moses, Aaron and Miriam"

(Mic 6:4).

Deborah is called a "prophetess" in Judges 4:4 who was judging Israel at that time. An example of her prophesying is given.

> Now she sent and summoned Barak the son of Abinoam from Kedesh-naphtali, and said to him, "Behold, the LORD, the God of Israel, has commanded, 'Go and march to Mount Tabor, and take with you ten thousand men from the sons of Naphtali and from the sons of Zebulun. And I will draw out to you Sisera, the commander of Jabin's army, with his chariots and his many troops to the river Kishon, and I will give him into your hand" (Jdgs 4:6-7).

Evidently, Deborah was very conscious that she had received an actual message from God.

During the monarchical period the only "prophetess" mentioned is Huldah. After Hilkiah had found the book of the law and Shaphan had read it to King Josiah, the King told him to "Go, inquire of the Lord for me and the people and all Judah concerning the words of this book...." (2 Kgs 22:13). The contingent from the King went directly to Huldah. She gave this message:

> Thus says the Lord God of Israel, "Tell the men that sent you to me, thus says the Lord, 'Behold, I bring evil on this place and on its inhabitants, even all the words of The book which the King of Judah has read...'" (2 Kgs 22:15-20).

Evidently Huldah was conscious that God spoke through her. Other prophetesses are mentioned, but no clear example of their message is mentioned. It is not clear whether Isaiah's wife is called a "prophetess" because of her relation to him or because she prophesied from God (Isa 8:3). The Lord through Ezekiel condemned "the daughters" who prophesied falsely, although in the same chapter he condemned the false male prophets (Eze 13). After the exile one of the detractors of Nehemiah was "Noadiah the prophetess" who with "the rest of the prophets were trying to frighten me" (Neh 6:14).

From the foregoing it is safe to conclude that the Old Testament legislation and practice indicated a rather wide participation of women in religious roles and activities. There were, however, certain restrictions on their participation, and they were not obligated to certain requirements on men. Their role in the prophetic ministry seems to be the exception and not the rule. Yet in every stage of the Old Testament history women participate, though in a lesser degree, in all the religious functions and privileges allowed to men. There is one exception, however. The priesthood began and remained as a solely male responsibility throughout. For further study see the excellent volume by Vos (1968) and the summary article by Waltke (1995) in the bibliography.

Woman's Religious Role in Second Temple Judaism

Although the Old Testament scriptures greatly influenced the thought patterns and customs of Jesus' time, the Rabbis' teaching had the greatest influence on patterns of thought and behavior. Their oral instruction did not begin to be written down until the end of the second century A.D. However, the Mishna and Talmud preserve attitudes that were prevalent hundreds of years before. Therefore, the later Talmudic teaching about women is representative of the general thrust of Jewish thought on this subject during Jesus' ministry. One might expect a "liberalizing" of restrictions with the passing of time. "Judaism, however, involves more of a reaction than progress" (Oepke, 781).

The general attitude toward women in Jesus' day was

that they were a necessary evil. They were considered inferior intellectually and religiously and were to be shunned socially. A sample of quotations from the Talmud may illustrate this attitude.

> The world cannot exist without males and females—happy is he whose children are males, and woe to him whose children are females (Talmud, *Kiddushin* 82b).

> Ten kabs of gossip descended to the world: nine were taken by women, and one by the rest of the world (Talmud *Erubin* 49b)

> Did not the sages say this: Engage not in much talk with women (*Erubin* 53b). Engage not in too much conversation with women. They said this in regard to one's own wife. How much more does the rule apply with regard to another man's wife. Hence have the sages said: As long as a man engages in too much conversation with women, he causes evil to himself, for he goes idle from the study of the Torah, so that his end will be that he will inherit gehenna (Mishna *Avot*, I, 5).

This strong indictment against conversing publicly with women explains the disciples' utter amazement at Jesus' conversing with the Samaritan woman in John 4:27.

Characteristic of the traditional position and estimation of women is a saying current in different forms among the Persians, Greeks and Jews. The Greeks traced it to Thales, Socrates, and Plato (Oepke, 777). The rabbis traced the saying to Rabbi Jehuda ben Elai who flourished around 150 A D.

It was taught: R. Jehuda used to say, a man is bound to say the following three blessings daily: "Blessed art thou who has not made me a heathen, who has not made me a woman, and who has not made me a brutish man" (*Menachot* 43b).

Many Jewish writers down through the years have sought to temper the harshness of these sentiments by affirming that in context the privileges of Jewish manhood are being cited and all that Rabbi Jehuda meant was that he was thankful that he had the opportunities of enjoying these privileges which he could not enjoy if he was a woman. However, no amount of explanation can erase the words or the fact that they are still found in the modern Jewish prayer book edited by E. Cohen with the consoling addition for women: "Praised be thou, Eternal One, Lord of the World, who has made me according to thy will" (cited by Oepke, 777).

One group of "restrictions" placed on women was given no doubt out of consideration for her domestic responsibilities. She was subject to all the negative prohibitions of the Torah (except for the three relating only to men: Lev 19:27; 21:1- 2), and to all the civil and penal legislation, including the penalty of death. However, as to the positive commandments of the Torah, the legal ruling is: "The observance of all the positive ordinances that depend on the time of the year is incumbent on men but not on women" (*Kiddushin* 1:7). In other words, women were exempt from commands of "Thou shalt," but not from the commands of "Thou shalt not." The "thou shalt" commands that depend on a definite point of time might interfere with domestic obligations. For example, the woman was not held responsible (1) to make a pilgrimage to Jerusalem at the festivals of Passover, Pentecost, and Tabernacles; (2) to live in booths during Tabernacles; (3) to shake the *lulav* during Tabernacles; (4) to sound the shofar at the New Year; (5) to read the *Megillah* at the Feast of Purim; and (6) to recite the daily *Shema.* [2]

Although the Old Testament commanded both men and women to hear the instruction of the law and has many examples of both men and women hearing the law (Deut 31:10-12; Josh 8:35; Neh 8:2-3), the Talmud issues strong prohibitions against women being taught.

> May the words of Torah be burned, than that they should be handed over to women. R. Eliezer says: "Whoever teaches his daughter Torah teaches her obscenity" (*Sota* 10a).

> If a man gives his daughter a knowledge of the law it is as though he taught her lechery (M. *Sota* 3, 4).

The motive behind these statements could be that women possessed more inferior intellectual capabilities than men. However, the Rabbis differed on this point. This prohibition grew more out of conviction that the Jewish woman was destined to be a homemaker. If she spent her time in study, her care of the household would suffer. As one Rabbi said to Rabbi Hiyya,

> Whereby do women earn merit? By making their children to go to the synagogue to learn Scripture and their husbands to the Beth Hamidrash to learn Mishna, and waiting for their husbands till they return from the Beth Hamidrash (*Berakot* 17a).

Whenever a Jewish woman did attend the temple or

---

[2] Joachim Jeremias, *Jerusalem in the Time of Jesus,* trans. F. H. and C. H. Cave (Philadelphia: Fortress Press, 1969), 372-373.

synagogue, certain restrictions were placed on her freedom. According to Josephus women could go no further in the Temple than into the Courts of the Gentiles and of the Women. There were three main courts of the second temple. Speaking of the second court, Josephus says:

> Through which court those of us who were ritually clean used to pass with our wives. Within this (second) court was the sacred court which women were forbidden to enter, and still further within was a third court into which only priests were permitted to go.[3]

It is interesting to observe that there was no "Court of the Women" in the First Temple, whose arrangement was given by God. Israelite lay-women had as much privilege as laymen in that structure. Both, of course, were not permitted in the *hekhal*, the main room for divine service.[4]

In the synagogue, of course, there were no separate courts for Gentiles, women, men, and priests. However, a similar restriction was placed on the presence of women – an arrangement that the first century writer Philo mentions. "In the synagogues women are assigned to special places behind a screen. Special chambers are provided for them."[5] In later years a gallery was built for them with a special entrance. These two sections were called a *sabbateion* (σαββατεῖον) and an *andron* (ἀνδρων). The first was open to women; the second was open only to men and boys, as the name suggests.[6]

---

[3] Flavius Josephus, *Antiquities* 15, 418, 419.

[4] *Encyclopedia Judaica, s.v. "Temple"* by Bezalel Narkiss.

[5] Philo Judaeus, *In Flaccum*, 89.

[6] Jeremias, 373.

Just as a strong restriction was placed on women being taught, an equally strong restriction was placed on women teaching. "An unmarried man must not be an elementary teacher (teacher of children), nor may a woman be an elementary teacher" (M. *Kiddushin*, iv. 13). This restriction extended also to the public reading of the Torah in synagogue.

> Our Rabbis taught: All are qualified to be among the seven (who read on the Sabbath), even a minor and a woman, only the sages said that a woman should not read the Torah out of respect to the congregation (*Megillot* 23a).

This stringent limitation on a woman's oral religious communication extended even to the sacred precincts of the home. In an interesting discussion in the Mishna, it is maintained that if three persons have eaten together, one of them should pronounce a benediction after the meal. However, "women, children, and slave may not be counted in the three" (M. *Berachot*, vii, 2).

Although it does not refer to any religious right or responsibility, one further restriction on women should be mentioned due to the bearing it has on a later discussion. In Judaism a woman had no right to bear witness in a judicial case. Her rights in this regard were no better than that of a slave.

> For that he (the slave) is disqualified from giving evidence can be learned by means of an *a fortiori* from the law in the case of women. For if a woman who is ineligible to enter into the congregation is yet ineligible to give evidence, how much more must a slave who is not eligible to enter into the congregation be ineligible to give evidence.

> Though she (the woman) is subject to the commandments she is disqualified from giving evidence (*Baba Kamma* 88a).

Josephus offered a reason for this exclusion due to the inherent instability of a woman. "Let not the testimony of women be admitted because of the levity and boldness of their sex."[7] Such a remark does not deserve any comment.

These burdensome restrictions certainly went far beyond what the Old Testament taught about women. It is certainly true that in many areas of life, Rabbinic Judaism involved more reaction than progress. When viewed against this rigid and barren background, the attitude of Jesus and the apostles toward women truly arrives as a welcome breath of fresh air!

---

[7] Josephus, *Antiquities* 4, 219.

WAS JESUS A FEMINIST?

Against the background of first century Palestinian Judaism, the attitude of Jesus toward women stands out boldly in contrast. His teachings about them and His actions toward them differed radically from the contemporary Rabbinic authorities. Although this contrast has been noted by many, an article by Leonard Swidler has served to open up the question as it relates to woman's place in church and society today.[8] Swidler seeks to prove that Jesus truly was a feminist in His attitudes and actions expressed in the Gospel accounts. He begins with his definition of a "feminist."

> By a feminist is meant a person who is in favor of, and who promotes, the equality of woman with men, a person who advocates and practices treating women primarily as human persons (as men are so treated) and willingly contravenes social customs in so acting. To prove the thesis it must be demonstrated that, so far as we can tell, Jesus neither said or did anything which would indicate that he advocated treating women as intrinsically inferior to men, but that on the contrary he said and did things which indicated that he thought of women as equals of men, and that in the process he willingly violated pertinent social mores.[9]

---

[8] Leonard Swidler, "Jesus was a Feminist," (*Catholic World*, January, 1971), 177-83.

[9] Swidler, 177.

The successful proof of a thesis depends greatly on how one defines the terms of the thesis. No evaluation of Swidler's definition of "feminist" will be given here. It should be noted, however, that he makes no distinction between "intrinsic inferiority" and "functional subordination." This distinction is very important as the examples of Jesus and Paul are analyzed.

That Jesus willingly violated social mores regarding women is evident. The position of women in His day was rather bleak, as has been noted in chapter one. An examination of Jesus' oral teaching reveals that He did not sympathize with the harsh attitude prevalent during His time. He contradicted and corrected many of the false notions regarding women held by His hearers. An examination of Jesus' actions reveals that He did willingly contravene certain unfair and unscriptural social customs and taboos regarding women.

Jesus' Attitude Toward Women
as Expressed in His Teaching

In a section of the Sermon on the Mount Jesus sought to correct prevalent false ideas regarding the law. Some of these false ideas related to several of the Ten Commandments.

> You have heard that it was said, "You shall not commit adultery"; but I say to you, that everyone who looks on a woman to lust for her has committed adultery with her already in his heart (Matt 5:27-28).

Jesus did not limit adultery to the physical act, but He points out the inward, spiritual attitude of "lust" as sin and a breach of the command in Exodus 20:14. Women were not regarded by Jesus as sex objects, i.e., simply as pieces of property to be used for physical gratification. They were to be respected as persons, not viewed as outlets for sexual drives. Jesus' attitude in this regard should be contrasted with what was permitted in ancient Israel.

> When you go out to battle against your enemies, and the LORD your God delivers them into your hands, and you take them away captive, and see among the captives a beautiful woman, and have a desire for her and would take her as a wife for yourself, then you shall bring her home to your house, and she shall shave her head and trim her nails. She shall also remove the clothes of her captivity and shall remain in your house, and mourn her father and mother a full month; and after that you may go in to her and be her husband and she shall be your wife. And it shall be, if you are not pleased with her, then you shall let her go wherever she wishes; but you shall certainly not sell her for money, you shall not mistreat her, because you have humbled her (Deut 21:10-14).

The last act does not mollify the harsh attitude allowed in treating a woman in such a way. Jesus' teaching in Matthew 5:27-28 served as a corrective for any such lingering notions in His day. Whatever rights a woman has, she has the right of respect in such matters.

Jesus' teaching on the right of divorce also contrasted with what Moses allowed in Matthew 19:3-9:

> And some Pharisees came to Him, testing Him, and saying, "Is it lawful for a man to divorce his wife for any cause at all?" And He answered and said, "Have you not read, that He who created them from the

beginning made them male and female, and said, 'For this cause a man shall leave his father and mother, and shall cleave to his wife; and the two shall become one flesh.' Consequently, they are no more two, but one flesh, what therefore God has joined together, let no man separate." They said to Him, "Why did Moses command to give her a certificate and divorce her?" He said to them, "Because of your hardness of heart, Moses permitted you to divorce your wives; but from the beginning it has not been this way. "And I say to you, whoever divorces his wife, except for immorality, and marries another woman commits adultery"

The Old Testament reference is Deuteronomy 24:1-4 which deals with a situation in which a husband divorces his wife after he has found some "indecency" (*ervat davar* - עֶרְוַת דָּבָר) in her, and what should be the action of her former husband if her second husband dies. It is not within the scope of this book to discuss the interpretations and problems related to these passages and other questions involving divorce and remarriage. However, what is pertinent to our subject is Jesus' refreshing attitude on how a woman should be respected, and not treated as a piece of property that can be discarded at will. The effect which this "new" teaching had on first-century Jewish attitudes is best reflected in the disciples' immediate reaction to Jesus' words, "If the relationship of the man and his wife is like this, it is better not to marry" (Matt 19:10). The disciples at this time had a long way to go in adjusting their views to the views of Jesus.

Twice in His ministry Jesus used the example of Gentile women in the Old Testament to rebuke the faithless of His own generation. In His synagogue sermon in His hometown of Nazareth, Jesus referred to a woman to illustrate that a prophet is not welcome in His own country.

> But I say to you in truth, there were many
> widows in Israel in the days of Elijah, when
> the sky was shut up for three years and six
> months, when a great famine came over all
> the land; and yet Elijah was sent to none of
> them, but only to Zarephath, in the land of
> Sidon, to a woman who was a widow
> (Luke 4:25-26).

That a woman should receive Elijah's ministry, and a Gentile woman at that, must have been a great rebuke to Jesus' male Jewish audience. They rose up in rage and attempted to murder Him (Luke 4:28-29).

Later in his ministry Jesus cited another female character in the Old Testament who would have eschatological significance.

> The Queen of the South shall rise up with
> the men of this generation at the judgment
> and condemn them, because she came
> from the ends of the earth to hear the
> wisdom of Solomon; and behold,
> something greater than Solomon is here.
> (Luke 11:31).

Jesus did not look on women, even Old Testament women, as unable to discern spiritual reality. If she recognized God's blessing on Solomon, how much greater is the guilt of those who refuse to recognize God working in and through the one "greater than Solomon." It is striking that Jesus' statement is that in the judgment she will condemn the "men" (*andron* - ἀνδρῶν) of this generation. Jesus included women in His parabolic teaching, and usually in a most favorable light. When He desired to teach His disciples to pray and to lose heart, He told the following parable.

23

> There was in a certain city a judge who did
> not fear God, and did not respect man.
> And there was a widow in that city, and she
> kept coming to him, saying, "Give me legal
> protection from my opponent." And for a
> while he was unwilling; but afterward he
> said to himself, "Even though I do not fear
> God nor respect man, yet because this
> widow bothers me, I will give her legal
> protection, lest by continually coming she
> wear me out." And the Lord said, "Hear
> what the unrighteous judge said; now shall
> not God bring about justice for His elect,
> who cry to Him day and night, and will He
> delay long over them? I tell you that He
> will bring about justice for them speedily.
> However, when the Son of Man comes,
> will He find faith on the earth?" (Luke
> 18:2-8).

The argument of the parable is from the lesser to the greater.
If an unjust judge listens to the cries of this woman, how much
more will our righteous father hear and respond to the cries of
the elect? However, Jesus presents this woman as a paragon
of virtue in contrast with a man who did not fear God. Since
Jesus' ministry was to the oppressed, He often favored the
widow, who was one of the most oppressed persons of His
day (Luke 4:18; Luke 20:45-47). To present in the same parable
a contrast between a commendable woman and an
unrighteous man must have been a departure from the way in
which women were normally considered during Jesus' time.

In Luke 15 Jesus presented three related problems.
Each parable was prompted by the criticism of the Pharisees
and the scribes regarding His eating with sinners. To show
that God Himself actively seeks sinners and rejoices when they
come to Him, Jesus related the parables of the shepherd and
his lost sheep, the woman and the lost coin, and the father and

the lost son. Each of them rejoiced when they found what they lost and called their friends and neighbors to rejoice with them. The truth illustrated is, "In the same way, I tell you, there is joy in the presence of the angels of God over one sinner who repents" (Luke 15:7,10). In the second parable the woman represents God. Much is made of this point by writers promoting the unqualified equality of men with women in all areas. If God is feminine, why cannot women represent Him in Christian ministry? This is hard to follow from such a parabolic teaching. Such exegesis also results in the conclusion that these three parables teach the Trinity, with the woman representing the Holy Spirit!

> ... this passage would seem to be particularly apt for Trinitarian interpretations: the prodigal son's father is God the Father (this interpretation has in fact been quite common in Christian history); since Jesus elsewhere identified himself as the Good Shepherd, the shepherd seeking the lost sheep is Jesus, the Son (this standard interpretation is reflected in, among other things, the often seen picture of Jesus carrying the lost sheep on His shoulders); the woman who sought the lost coin should "logically" be the Holy Spirit. If such an interpretation has existed, it surely has not been common. Should such lack of "logic" be attributed to the general cultural denigration of women or the abhorrence of pagan goddesses – although Christian abhorrence of pagan gods did not result in a Christian rejection of a male image of God?[10]

---

[10] Swidler, 183.

This type of exegesis of a parable to "prove" a point is its own refutation. While it is obvious that the woman represents God in the parable it should be noted that He pictures her in quite a typical womanly duty – cleaning the house! Such an observation would be abhorrent to the feminists.

Jesus' Attitude Toward Women as Expressed in His Actions

Although certain indications of Jesus' attitude toward women can be discerned from His teaching, a greater appreciation of His view of women can be gathered from how He acted in their presence. Jesus made no feminist pronouncements of equality. Although He sharply contrasted His own teachings with those of the Jewish leaders of His day, He never did this when it came to the question of woman's place in religion and society. He never clashed with the religious leaders about women's rights as He did about other subjects. However, the way He acted toward women surely was different from the typical male behavior of that day.

> It was not so much in what He said as in how he related to women that Jesus was a revolutionary. In this relationship his own lifestyle was so remarkable that one can only call it astonishing. He treated women as fully human, equal to men in every respect; no word of deprecation about women, as such, is ever found on his lips. As the Savior who identified with the oppressed and the disinherited, he talked to women and about women with complete freedom and candor.[11]

---

[11]Paul K. Jewett, *Man as Male and Female* (Eerdmans, 1975).

Jesus consciously and deliberately contravened many Rabbinic taboos regarding women. He did this publicly and privately, and sometimes He caused public and private reaction to His behavior.

Jesus ministered to women <u>physically</u>. In each of the three cases of His raising someone from the dead, a woman is closely related to the scene. The raising of Jairus' daughter is recorded in all three synoptic gospels (Matthew 9:18-26; Mark 5:22-43; Luke 8:41-56). Although touching a dead corpse would have made Him ritually unclean according to Numbers 19:11-21, Jesus did not hesitate to take her by the hand and say, "Child, arise!" (Luke 8:54). Luke also records the touching scene of Jesus raising the only son of the widow of Nain.

> And when the Lord saw her, He felt compassion for her, and said to her, "Do not weep." And He came up and touched the coffin; and the bearers came to a halt. And He said, "Young man, I say to you, arise!" And the dead man sat up, and began to speak. And Jesus gave him back to his mother (Luke 7:12-15).

The centrality of the woman as the focus of Jesus' compassion is evident from the narrative. The third person Jesus raised from the dead was Lazarus of Bethany, brother of Mary and Martha. It was to Martha that He made one of the astounding revelations of His person and work that are recorded in the Gospel of John.

> Martha therefore, when she heard that Jesus was coming, went to meet Him; but Mary still sat in the house. Martha therefore said to Jesus, "Lord, if You had been here, my brother would not have died. "Even now I know that whatever You ask of God, God will give You." Jesus said to her, "Your brother shall rise

27

again." Martha said to Him, "I know that he will rise again in the resurrection on the last day." Jesus said to her, "I am the resurrection and the life; he who believes in Me shall live even if he dies, and everyone who lives and believes in Me shall never die. Do you believe this?" She said to Him, "Yes, Lord; I have believed that You are the Christ, the Son of God, *even* He who comes into the world" (John 11:20-27).

Jesus did not hesitate to instruct a woman in the deepest truths regarding His person. He did not consider her unable to comprehend spiritual realities. She herself gave one of the most fervent confessions of Jesus' Messiahship that is found in the Gospel history.

Jesus ministered physically to other women. He healed Peter's mother-in-law, (Mark 1:30-31) and straightened a woman bent for eighteen years, also calling her "a daughter of Abraham" (Luke 7:11-17). The most striking example of Jesus' healing of women was His deliverance of the woman who had been hemorrhaging for twelve years (Matt 9:20-22; Mark 5:25-34: Luke 8:43-48). Perhaps this discharge of blood was a menstrual flow (as some have assumed[12]), but it is clear from Leviticus 15:19-33 that she was considered ritually unclean and rendered unclean anyone she touched. Jesus did not rebuke her for touching Him. When she fell down before Him, His loving word was, "Daughter, your faith has made you well, go in peace, and be healed of your affliction" (Mark 5:34). Although it may appear that Jesus' public display of the embarrassed woman may have resulted in some psychological discomfort for her, His purpose was an evident dramatic

---

[12] Letha Scanzoni and Nancy Hardesty, *All We're Meant To Be* (Waco, Texas: Word Books, 1974), 57.

display of this lesson about the dignity of women.

Jesus also ministered to women spiritually. Three incidents in the Gospel are illustrative of His practice of not fearing to teach women spiritual truths. The first of these occurred on the Lord's journey from Judea to Galilee when He passed through Samaria (John 4:1-42). While he was sitting by Jacob's well in Sychar, a person approached who had three negative attributes by the standards of the day. The person was a woman, a harlot, and a Samaritan. When Jesus initiated a conversation with her, it was much to her surprise, because the conducting of the conversation was a breach of "acceptable" male behavior in those days.

> Jose b. Johanan of Jerusalem used to say: "Engage not in too much conversation with women. … As long as a man engages in too much conversation with women, he causes evil to himself, for he goes idle from the study of the Torah, so that his end will be to inherit Gehenna" (*Abot* I, 5).

That such a breach of social behavior took place is evident from the reaction of the disciples when they returned and discovered what Jesus had been doing.

> "At this point His disciples came, and they were amazed that He had been speaking with a woman, yet no one said, 'What do You seek?' or, 'Why do You speak with her'?" (John 4:27).

If conversing publicly with a woman was not enough of a breach of accepted social behavior, teaching her publicly certainly was. This is evident from a number of later rabbinic sources (*Sota* 10a, 21b; *M. Sota* iii, 4, cited earlier). However, Jesus taught her about the nature of God and His worship. He also gave her the earliest revelation of his Messiahship.

> The woman said to Him, "I know that
> Messiah is coming (He who is called
> Christ); when that One comes, He will
> declare all things to us." Jesus said to her,
> "I who speak to you am *He*" (John 4:25-
> 26).

This woman testified about her encounter with Jesus and many Samaritans eventually believed on Him because of her word (John 4:28-30; 39-42). Jesus willingly contravened custom to bring the "water of life" to this needy woman.

A second incident with a woman, although lacking in some of the major Greek manuscripts[13], probably does preserve an actual historical occurrence. The scribes and Pharisees brought a woman to Jesus who had been discovered in the very act of adultery. When they said, "Now in the Law Moses commanded us to stone such women," (John 4:5) they were also betraying a misunderstanding of what Moses said.

> If there is a girl who is a virgin engaged to
> a man, and another finds her in the city and
> lies with her, then you shall bring them
> both out to the gate of that city and you
> shall stone them to death; the girl, because
> she did not cry out in the city, and the
> man because he has violated his neighbor's
> wife. Thus you shall purge the evil from
> among you (Deut 22:23-24).

It is not mentioned if this woman was a "virgin engaged," and it is obvious that they were not interested in doing all that Moses commended, for the absence of the guilty man is

---

[13] John 7:53-8:11 is not found in p66, p75, ℵ, A, B, C, and seven additional majuscule manuscripts.

evident. Jesus, however, refused to fall into the snare of denying the Mosaic law, but simply responded, "He who is without sin among you, let him be the first to throw a stone at her" (John 8:7). Of course, Jesus did not condone the woman's act, as much as He condemned this example of hypocritical arrogance. His gentle admonition was simply, "Neither do I condemn you; go your way; from now on sin no more" (John 8:11).

On His first recorded visit to the house of Mary, Martha and Lazarus in Bethany, Jesus showed His appreciation of the intellectual and spiritual capacity of women (Luke 10:33-42). While Martha was busily engaged in household chores and cooking,

> Mary sat attentively at the Lord's feet, listening to his teaching. When Martha complained because Mary was not helping her, Jesus gently rebukes her, "Martha, Martha, you are worried and bothered about so many things; but only a few things are necessary, really only one: for Mary has chosen the good part, which shall not be taken away from her" (Luke 10:41-42).

The one "thing" that is absolutely necessary is the care of the spiritual life, and Jesus commended and did not discourage Mary in her desire. Although it seems to be tenuous to use this account as a basis for a woman's studying theology for the ministry, as some have done,[14] it certainly is an indication of Jesus' regard for a woman's capability intellectually and spiritually. It certainly is not, however, a downgrading of the "home-ministry" of women, and to affirm such reflects a total

---

[14] Virginia Mollenkott, "Church Women, Theologians, and the Burden of Proof," *Reformed Journal*, vol. 25, number 7.

misunderstanding of Jesus' words.[15]

Not only did Jesus minister to women physically, hut women also ministered to Him in various ways. He attracted their ministry and their sincere expression of love. There was some pure attraction that He manifested. When Jesus traveled, His entourage of supporters included women.

> And it came about soon afterwards, that He began going about from one city and village to another, proclaiming and preaching the Kingdom of God; and the twelve were with Him and also some of the women who had been healed of evil spirits and sicknesses: Mary who was called Magadalene from whom seven demons had gone out, and Joanna the wife of Chuza, Herod's steward, and Susanna, and many others contributed to their support out of their private means (Luke 8:1-3).

These women had been healed by Jesus, and out of grateful love, they ministered to Him and His disciples. Theirs was a different honor from that of the other followers of Jesus. Many others had received from Him; these had the privilege of "ministering" to Him in return. The word in verse 3 translated "contributed" in the New American Standard Bible is *diekonoun* (διηκόνουν). The occurrences of this word and its cognates in the gospels indicate that whenever such ministry is rendered directly to Jesus, it is either by angels or women. After the temptation in the wilderness, "angels came and began to minister (*diekonoun* - διηκόνουν) to Him" (Matt 4:11). After her healing, Peter's mother-in-law "arose and began to wait (*diekonei* - διηκόνει) on Him" (Matt 8:15).

Evidently, these women who followed Jesus were of some substance. Jesus attracted followers from both the poor

---

[15] Scanzoni and Hardesty, 56.

and the rich classes. This is the only passage in the gospels which tells how Jesus and His disciples lived when they were not being entertained by hospitable persons. The devoted love of these female followers was not temporary. At the hour of his greatest need, His male disciples "all left Him and fled" (Mark 14:50). Who was it that stayed by Him in faithful devotion throughout the gruesome ordeal of crucifixion?

> And there were also some women looking on from afar, among whom were Mary Magdalene, and Mary the mother of James the Less and Jesus, and Salome. And when He was in Galilee, they used to follow Him and minister (*diekonoun* - διηκόνουν) to him; and there were many other women who had come up with Him to Jerusalem (Mark 15:40-41).

Their devotion to Him was not exhausted by their monetary contributions. Even beyond the cross they devotedly continued to follow the one who had healed their spirits and bodies.

> Now the women who had come with Him out of Galilee followed after, and saw the tomb and how His body was laid. And they returned and prepared spices and perfumes. And on the Sabbath they rested according to the commandment (Luke 23:55-56).

All four gospels indicate clearly that it was women who were first to receive the news of the Lord's resurrection (Matt 28:1; Mark 16:1; Luke 24:1; John 20:1). They were the first actual witnesses of Jesus in His resurrected body (Matt 28:9; Mark 16:9; John 20:14-17). Their choice as witnesses has great significance, since the testimony of women was not allowed in legal decisions in those days (see earlier Rabbinic references).

The disciples reflected this first-century attitude in their unbelieving skepticism at the women's report (Mark 16:11; Luke 24:11; John 20:3-10, esp. v.9). Their unbelief was due greatly to their spiritual insensitivity to what Jesus had already told them about his resurrection, but their male prejudice cannot be discounted either.

Why is it that women like these loved Him so much that they followed Him with sacrificial, and probably unpopular devotion? Why is it that a formerly immoral woman could cry tears of thanks on Jesus' feet and dry them with her hair without fear of rebuke (Luke 7:36-50)? Why is it that Mary felt so free in his presence and would anoint His feet with costly perfume (John 12:1-8)? Let a male and female give their answers to these questions.

> Jesus simply accepts these women as persons: compassionately and with complete purity and simplicity he accepts their affection while moving them to repentance. Thus he establishes at once God's judgment on their standards of life and his mercy towards them.[16]

> Perhaps it is no wonder that the women were first at the Cradle and last at the Cross. They had never known a man like this Man – there never has been such another. A prophet and teacher who never nagged at them, never flattered or coaxed or patronized; who never made arch (i.e., mischievous) jokes about them, never treated them either as "The women, God help us!" or "The ladies, God bless them!";

---

[16] C.F. D. Moule, *The Phenomenon of the New Testament* (London: SCM Press LTD, 1967), 65.

who rebuked without querulousness and praised without condescension; who took their questions and arguments seriously; who never mapped out their sphere for them, never urged them to be feminine or jeered at them for being female; who had no axe to grind and no uneasy male dignity to defend; who took them as he found them and was completely unselfconscious. There is no act, no sermon, no parable in the whole Gospel that borrows its pungency from female perversity; nobody could possibly guess from the words and deeds of Jesus that there was anything "funny" about women's nature.[17]

So Was Jesus a Feminist?

After this survey of Jesus' attitude toward women as expressed in His teaching and His actions, that question must still be answered. It is needless to affirm again that His attitude differed radically from the typical attitude of first-century Pharisaic Judaism. He treated women as persons, as spiritual equals with men, and capable of intellectual and spiritual comprehension. Jesus did not believe in the inherent inferiority of the female sex. If that is the essence of feminism, then Jesus was a feminist. However, feminism does not include a belief in the possibility of diverse functions for the male and the female. As it pertains to religion and the church, which is the particular concern of this book, feminism affirms the equal opportunity for women in all functions of ministry,

---

[17] Dorothy Sayers, *Are Women Human?* (Grand Rapids: Wm. B. Eerdmans Publishing Co., 1971), 47.

including ordination as priests, pastors and elders. There are evangelicals who claim to affirm the full integrity of Scripture who also believe that the Scripture warrants such a privilege for women.[18] Although a fuller discussion of this position is reserved for later, here it is noted that these writers claim Jesus' teaching and actions as being fully supportive of their conclusions. Can the ministry of Jesus be regarded as supporting women's full ordination as pastors?

Regarding their spiritual privileges, Jesus taught equality between men and women. However, regarding their spiritual function and activity, He did recognize a distinction. In this regard, it is interesting to note what He did <u>not</u> do, as much as what he <u>did</u> do. Is it not significant that no woman was chosen among the twelve (Matt 10:1-4; Mark 3:13-15)? It was to these men that the apostolic commissions were given (John 20:19-23; Matt 28:16-20). Mollenkott scoffs at using this fact as an argument against a female preaching ministry.

> Such argumentation is embarrassing to deal with…. Not only does the argument about male apostles ignore the fact that no one would have listened to women had they been appointed as Christ's ambassadors since first-century men ignored women in public, ruled women ineligible as witnesses in courts of law, and considered women ritually unclean at least one quarter of their lives; it also ignores the

---

[18] Mollenkott, 18; Jewett, 103, 160-170; Nancy Hardesty, "Women: Second Class Citizens?," *Eternity*, January, 1971, 14-16, 24-29; Donald W. and Lucille Sider Dayton, "Women as Preachers: Evangelical Precedents," *Christianity Today*, May 23, 1975, 4-7; Richard Quebedeaux, *The Young Evangelicals* (New York: Harper and Row Publishers, 1974), 109-114. See also the recent volumes by Payne and Westfall in the Bibliography.

fact that the apostles were not only male, but Jewish! If we are to be literal about the sex of the apostles as norms for Christian leadership, then let us be equally literal about their ethnic backgrounds: all priests and ministers and church leaders must be Jewish converts to Christianity!... Neither the ethnic nor the sexual restriction can logically be applied to candidates for the modern clergy, nor can Christ's choice of twelve Jewish men be regarded as normative in keeping women subordinate in the church.[19]

The problem with Mollenkott's argument is that it conveniently ignores the truth it affirms. Jesus **was** willing to ignore the oppressive social restrictions on women in His ministry. He **was** bold and "revolutionary" in doing for them what would have been frowned on by male contemporaries. If a feminist is one who "willingly contravenes social customs" in promoting "the equality of women with men,"[20] and Jesus was a true feminist, then He would not be hesitant to appoint six females and six males as His apostles, if He had so wished. To say otherwise is to charge Him with the fear of man; a characteristic He never showed in His other "revolutionary" dealings with women. To affirm that Jesus commissioned women to preach when He commanded them to bear the news of His resurrection to the disciples ignores what Jesus again did not do. "Then Jesus said to them, 'Do not be afraid, go and take word to my brethren to leave for Galilee, and there they shall see Me'" (Matt 28:10). Jesus did not command them to witness to the world but to His "brothers." To them He

---

[19] Mollenkott, 18.

[20] Swidler, 177. Swidler expanded his arguments in his later work: *Women in the Ministry of the New Testament* (1980).

gave the commission to bear the Gospel message to all the world. Of course, Jesus never forbade a woman to testify what He had done for her, as the Samaritan woman did for those in her village (John 4:28-30, 39-42). Nevertheless, while encouraging such testifying, He never chose a woman for official public ministry.[21]

We should not look to Jesus' ministry for detailed examples of what a woman can do for Christ. However, some indications can be gathered from how women ministered to Him and how He accepted their ministry.

> In the life of our Lord women had a very special place as ministers to Him in a sense in which no man was His minister. This ministry consisted of caring for His physical needs, by giving of money, and preparing spices for His dead body. Jesus allowed the women to follow Him, He taught them, and He honored them with the first announcement of His resurrection. But equally important, He also limited their activity by not choosing one of them for official work. Thus, we may say that, while Jesus granted great freedom to women and placed importance on their ministrations, He limited the sphere of their activity by glorifying the domestic responsibilities with which they ministered to Him.[22]

---

[21] On Jesus and women, see James Borland, "Women in the Life and Teachings of Jesus," *Recovering Biblical Manhood and Womanhood: A Response to Evangelical Feminism*. Eds. Piper and Grudem (Wheaton: Crossway, 1991), 113-23; and J.H. Elliott, "Jesus Was Not an Egalitarian," *Biblical Theology Bulletin* 32 (2002): 75-91.

[22] Charles Caldwell Ryrie, *The Role of Women in the Church* (Chicago: Moody Press, 1970), 38.

WAS PAUL A MISOGYNIST OR AN EGALITARIAN?

Attitudes towards Paul's "view of women" have ranged from utter disdain to warm admiration. He is sometimes viewed by modern feminists as expressing the epitome of male arrogance and misogyny ("hatred of women").

> Christian ideology has contributed no little to the oppression of woman....Through St. Paul the Jewish tradition, savagely antifeminist, was affirmed. St. Paul enjoyed self-effacement and discretion upon women; he based the subordination of woman to man upon both the Old and New Testaments....In a religion that holds the flesh accursed, woman becomes the devil's most fearsome temptation.[23]

> St. Paul, considered one of the prime women-haters of his day, said that man was not created for woman, but that woman was created for man. He also had a loathing of sex and said, "It is good for a man not to touch a woman." However, he recommended that people get married if they could not overcome their sexual instincts ("It is better to marry than to burn."). He also disliked women who spoke for themselves – especially when they disagreed with men. "Let the woman

---

[23] Simone de Beauvoir, *The Second Sex*, trans. By H. M. Paishley (New York: Alfred A. Knopf, 1975), 97.

learn in silence with all subjection," he declared. "Wives submit yourselves to your husbands." St. Paul's letter of instructions to the Corinthians established the place of woman – on the bottom. "The head of every man is Christ; and the head of the woman is the man," he told them.[24]

On the other hand, there are feminists who try to take the Scriptures seriously. Some of these writers view Paul as marvelously liberated in his vision of women, and a model example of a true egalitarian ("one that asserts the equality of mankind").

> And the magnificent affirmation that in Christ there is no male and female (Gal. 3:28) was, for the apostle, not merely a matter of theory. He acted out this truth in a most remarkable way, for a former rabbi. We may conclude, then, that Paul... by no means denied in his life style the implications of the truth that in Christ there is no male and female. Here he made only a beginning, to be sure, in implementing his insight. But it is high time that the church press on to the full implementation of the apostle's vision concerning the equality of the sexes in Christ.[25]

To adequately assess where the truth lies between these two extremes, it is necessary to examine the actual statements

---

[24] Lucy Komisar, *The New Feminism*, quoted by Richard S. Wheeler, *Pagans in the Pulpit* (New Rochelle, N.Y.: Arlington House, 1974), 68.

[25] Jewett, 147. See again Westfall's *Paul and Gender* (2016).

Paul made about women as well as how he acted toward them in his ministry. The latter endeavor will occupy much of the following chapter. However, since the concern of this work is with woman's role in the church, only those statements that relate directly to that issue will be examined in this chapter. His main statements that relate directly to the issues of public ministry are 1 Timothy 2:9-15; 1 Corinthians 14:33b-35; 1 Corinthians 11:2-16; and Galatians 3:28. The first two references are prohibitions that Paul makes on woman's role, and the latter two references are pronouncements that Paul makes on woman's position.

Pauline Prohibitions

1 Timothy 2:9-15

In this epistle, Paul is writing to instruct Timothy about the life of the church. He clearly expresses his purpose as follows:

> I am writing these things to you, hoping to come to you before long; but in case I am delayed, I write so that you will know how one ought to conduct himself in the household of God, which is the church of the living God, the pillar and support of the truth (1 Tim 3:14-15).

Chapter 2:1-8 particularly concerns prayer that is to be offered for all people, and concludes with the word, "Therefore, I want the men in every place to pray, lifting holy hands, without wrath and doubting." Then there follows the passage that contains a strong prohibition regarding women's teaching.

> Likewise, I want women to adorn themselves with proper clothing, modestly and discreetly, not with braided hair and gold or pearls or costly garments, but

rather by means of good works, as is
proper for women making a claim to
godliness. A woman must quietly receive
instruction with entire submissiveness. But
I do not allow a woman to teach or exercise
authority over a man, but to remain quiet.
For it was Adam who was first created, and
then Eve. And it was not Adam who was
deceived, but the woman being deceived,
fell into transgression. But women will be
reserved through the bearing of children if
they continue in faith and love and sanctity
with self-restraint (1 Tim 2:9-15).

This entire section of chapter two has to do with public
worship. Men are to pray "in every place," probably referring
to the various places of meeting. "Likewise" (*Hosautos* -
Ὡσαύτως) links the action of the men in verse 8 to that of the
women in verse 9. A verbal thought must be supplied to make
the sentence of verse 9 complete. The thought expressed can
be paraphrased in this way, "Likewise (I desire) the women
(when they pray) to adorn themselves…." Paul's desire is that
women should come to the public worship in "respectable
clothing" (*en katastole kosmio* - ἐν καταστολῇ κοσμίῳ), and their
whole deportment should be one of "modesty" (*aidous* -
αἰδοῦς) and "moderation" (*sophrosunes* - σωφροσύνης). Part of
this "moderate" deportment is care about ostentatious
clothing. Verse 9 ends with a warning against "braided hair
and gold or pearls or costly garments." The Greek indicates
that he is not condemning the simple braided hair common
throughout history. The connective *kai* (καὶ) between "braids"
(*plegamasin* - πλέγμασιν) and "gold" (*chrusio* - χρυσίῳ), indicates
that what Paul is forbidding refers to an ancient custom,
common to courtesans, of weaving gold into the hair.

In this fashion the hair is divided into

numerous small plaits or braids –at least eleven, and sometimes as many as twenty-five, but always an odd number – which are allowed to hang down the back. Into each of these braids, or thin plaited tresses of hair, three strings of black silk, some eighteen inches in length, are woven, to which an immense number of small gold spangles are fastened at irregular intervals. The countless gold spangles almost entirely hide the hair, and glitter and twinkle with every movement of the head. It would be difficult to find in the way of jewelry a vainer or more artificial form of female adornment.[26]

Such gaudy adornment is anything but modest and would distract the attention of other worshippers. That which is proper to a woman "who professes the fear of God" is found in verse 10, i.e., "good works." The purity of her actions and the example of her charity clothe her with a far more lasting apparel. Peter amplifies this point very well.

Your adornment must not be merely external: braiding the hair, and wearing gold jewelry, or putting on dresses; but let it be the hidden person of the heart, with the imperishable quality of a gentle and quiet spirit, which is precious in the sight of God (1 Pet 3:3-4).

Moving from her adornment to her attitude in the church meeting, verse 11 issues a general command relating to a woman's attitude to teaching. "Let a woman quietly receive

---

[26] James Neil, *Everyday Life in the Holy Land* (London: Cassell and Company, Limited, 1913), 200-201.

instruction with entire submissiveness." The closing phrase (*en pase hupotage* - ἐν πάσῃ ὑποταγῇ) can be paraphrased as "subordinating herself in every respect."[27] Thus the general attitude of the woman is that of subordination in every area. This general principle finds expression throughout the New Testament relating to both home and church (1 Cor 11:3, 8-9, 12; 14:34; Eph 5:22-33; Col 3:18; 1 Pet 3:1). Although this passage is often viewed as a harsh prohibition against woman's freedom, in Paul's day it was quite a breakthrough for women. As has been noted in Chapter One, during the NT period and later Jewish women were exempted from learning the Torah and remained in a screened-off room in the synagogue during the rare occasions when they were allowed to attend. That Paul allowed women to learn in silence at all was quite radical. It was a return to the original Deuteronomic command, "assemble the people, men, women, and little ones, and the sojourners within your towns, that they may hear and learn to fear the Lord your God..." (Deut 31:12).

After this command that a woman should learn in submission, Paul issues a negative prohibition in verse 12: "But I do not allow a woman to teach or exercise authority over a man, but to remain quiet." That which is forbidden to women is "teaching" (*didaskein* - διδάσκειν) and "exercising authority" (*authentein* - αὐθεντεῖν) over a "male" (*andros* - ἀνδρός). These are the two basic functions of an elder (*presbuteros* - πρεσβύτερος), which in NT usage is synonymous with a bishop or overseer (*episkopos* - ἐπίσκοπος).

> Let the elders who rule well be considered
> worthy of double honor, especially those
> who work hard at preaching and teaching
> (1 Tim 5:17; see also Matt 13:7, 17).

---

[27] W.F. Arndt, F.W. Gingrich, Frederick Danker, *A Greek-English Lexicon of the New Testament and Other Early Christian Literature*, 3rd ed (Chicago: Univ. of Chicago Press, 1990), 1041.

Immediately following the passage under consideration is the section of the epistle describing the characteristics of an overseer. "An overseer, then, must be above reproach, the husband of one wife, temperate, prudent, respectable, hospitable, able to teach (*didaktikon* - διδακτικόν)" (1 Tim 3:2). In forbidding to women the functions of teaching and exercising authority, Paul is denying to them the role of elder/bishop in a local congregation. In teaching men publicly, she is exercising authority over them. This public exercise of authority over men is the key in the apostle's thinking in all his writing about these matters, as we shall see later.

Some versions have re-introduced the idea that what Paul was forbidding is a woman usurping or assuming authority over a male elder, but this does not forbid authority, only its abuse of authority (see KJV: "usurp authority"). The NIV2011, for example, reads, "I do not permit a woman to teach or to *assume authority* over a man, she must be quiet." While the translation team professed to be complementarian, this translation may at least support the idea that women can exercise authority over men in church as long as they do not "assume" or "usurp" that authority. This interpretation of *authentein* - αὐθεντεῖν destroys the parallelism with the other infinitive, *didaskein* - διδάσκειν, which simply means "to teach." It also is not the meaning of the word. The most authoritative NT Greek lexicon glosses *authentein* as follows: "*to give orders to, to dictate to*...practically = 'tell a man what to do'."[28]

All the verbal forms in verse 12 are in the present tense. Notice of this is taken by a prominent egalitarian author.

> Note that Paul does not say "I will never allow or permit," but instead he says "I am not allowing or permitting." He wrote in the present active indicative tense.[29]

---

[28] BDAG, 150. See GE (Montonari), 337: "to have full authority."

Evidently Spencer construes the present tense as cause for taking Paul's "advice" on a purely temporary basis. In other words, "This is what I am *now* saying." This emphasis evidently leaves open the possibility of Paul's altering the prohibition at other times. Attempting to prove such a point from the present tense is a rather tenuous argument and can be answered by anyone having some familiarity with Greek grammar and tense usage. A.T. Robertson, for example, calls this use of the present tense the "Iterative or Customary Present."[30] This use of the present tense does not just describe a situation that is going on, but denotes a steady practice that is characteristic of the writer.[31] Thus Paul's idea can be expressed as: "It is my steady custom and practice not to allow women to be exercising the office of teacher and to be exercising the office of ruling over a man."

It should be noted again that the prohibition is not that a woman may not teach anyone, but that she should not teach and exercise authority over a man in the public life of the church. Examples of women teaching other women and children and another man privately appear in the New Testament (Tit 2:3-4; 1Tim 3:14-15; Acts 18:26). These examples, however, do not contradict the principle that Paul lays down. These and other examples of women's ministry will

---

[29] Aida Besancon Spencer, "Eve at Ephesus," in *Journal of the Evangelical Theological Society*, Vol. 17, No. 4 (Fall, 1974), 219.

[30] A.T. Robertson, *A Grammar of the Greek New Testament in the Light of Historical Research* (New York: Hodder and Stoughton, 1914), 8. D.B. Wallace, *Greek Grammar Beyond the Basics*, (Grand Rapids: Zondervan, 1996), 520-22.

[31] Other uses of the "Customary Present" are 1 Cor. 9:26: "Therefore I run (*trecho* - τρέχω) in such a way, as not without aim; I box (*pukteuo* - πυκτεύω) in such a way...," and Luke 18:12: "I fast (*nesteuo* - νηστεύω) twice a week; I pay tithes (*apodekato* - ἀποδεκατῶ) of all that I get."

be examined in the next chapter.

This strong prohibition in 2:12 was not an arbitrary decision by Paul based on ancient socio-cultural factors or in light of the local situation in Ephesus. He proceeds in 2:13-14 to give the theological reasons that form the basis of his restriction.

> For it was Adam who was first created, *and* then Eve. And *it was* not Adam who was deceived, but the woman being deceived, fell into transgression.

The reasons given are two-fold: 1. The priority of Adam in the creation; and 2. The priority of Eve in the fall.

A better translation of 2:13 is "For Adam was formed first (*protos* - πρῶτος), then (*eita* - εἶτα) Eve." The description of creation as a "forming" and the use of the sequential phrase "first . . . then" clearly illustrate that the passage Paul has in mind is Genesis 2. Genesis 2:7 reads: "Then the LORD God formed man of dust from the ground, and breathed into his nostrils the breath of life; and man became a living being." The word for "formed" in the LXX is *eplasen* (ἔπλασεν), the aorist active form of the same verb used by Paul in 1 Timothy 2:13. Subsequent to God's forming of Adam is the formation of Eve in Genesis 2:21-23.

> So the LORD God caused a deep sleep to fall upon the man, and he slept; then He took one of his ribs and closed up the flesh at that place. The LORD God fashioned into a woman the rib which He had taken from the man, and brought her to the man. The man said, "This is now bone of my bones, and flesh of my flesh; she shall be called Woman (*ishah* - אִשָּׁה), because she was taken out of Man (*ish* - אִישׁ)."

Paul grounds his argument on the clear teaching in Genesis that the woman derived her existence from the man. He explained this further in another context: "For man does not originate from woman, but woman from man; for indeed man was not created for the woman's sake, but woman for the man's sake" (1 Cor 11:8-9).

If the woman came into being for the man, then she is not to reverse that order by ruling over man. To do so would be a rejection of the purpose of God in her creation. She was created to "help" man and to be his companion, not to be his ruler (see Gen 2:18). To remark that today one cannot see what Paul sees in this account is to evade the point. That point is that an apostle views the creation order as significant for the role of women in the family and in the church. To question the apostle's conclusion is to involve oneself in another serious discussion with serious implications, i.e., whether or not that apostle was inspired to teach authoritatively! To comment that "the theological leap from this (the order of creation) to woman's subordination is a traditional rabbinic understanding that is not supported by the text" is to undercut apostolic authority on any scriptural interpretation and application that the apostle makes.[32]

The first reason that Paul gives in 1 Timothy 2:13 (the order of creation) probably relates more to his prohibition against a woman's "ruling over a man" in 2:12. The second reason that is given in 2:14 probably relates more to his prohibition against woman's "teaching a man" in 2:12. The translation of 2:14, therefore, should bring out the difference in Greek between the two words for "deceive." "And Adam was not deceived (*epatethe* - ἠπατήθη) but the woman being quite deceived (*exapatetheisa* - ἐξαπατηθεῖσα) was involved in the transgression." Paul, of course, is referring to the account of the fall in Genesis 3. Since he does not give the reason why Eve was approached and deceived first, it seems that it is going beyond the text to conclude that women are more gullible,

---

[32] For criticism of this view, see Scanzoni and Hardesty, 25-28.

more emotional, and less rational as some commentators do.[33] These characteristics may or may not be true, but they are not stated by the texts as the reason. Since Adam was as guilty as Eve in the disobedience, it would seem that these weak characteristics could apply to him as well (cf. also Rom 5:12ff). The real reason probably lies in Eve's rejection of her subordinate position by taking the lead instead of following. The different words for the deception of Eve and Adam may provide the best approach. It is again important to point out that Adam was not "deceived" (aorist of *apatao* - ἀπατάω), but Eve was "quite deceived" (participle of *exapatao* - ἐξαπατάω). They both sinned, and they both were culpable. However, Adam was not deceived in the manner in which Eve was deceived. "But I am afraid, lest as the serpent deceived (*exapatesen* - ἐξηπάτησεν) Eve" (2 Cor 11:3). She listened directly to Satan; he did not. She sinned before he did. She led when she should have followed.

The observations of a respected commentator on the entire NT are helpful in this regard.

> And now that which before was an unmixed blessing – namely, that Eve, by virtue of her creation, constantly followed Adam – is an unmixed blessing no longer; for now she who, by her sinful example, chose to rule him who at that moment was still her sinless husband, must obey the creature of her own designing, namely, her sinful husband. Hence, let none of her

---

[33] See, e.g., Albert Barnes: "She had evinced a readiness to yield to temptation; a feebleness of resistance; a pliancy of character which showed that she was not adapted to the situation of headship, and which made it proper that she should ever afterwards occupy a subordinate situation." See *Notes on Thessalonians – Philemon* (Grand Rapids: Baker, 1969), 137.

daughters follow her in reversing the divinely established order. Let none assume the role that was not intended for her. Let not the daughter of Eve teach, rule, lead when the congregation gathers for worship. Let her learn, not teach; obey, not rule; follow, not lead.[34]

The issue involved in 1 Timothy 2 is not an inherent inferiority of woman's intellectual and spiritual capabilities, but her function in ministry. She is not subordinate in her capability, but she is to be subordinate in her role. Let it also be noted clearly that Paul does not ground his reasoning in the male-dominated culture of his day. He does not write: "Women should not teach because men will not accept them as teachers." He grounds his teaching in the order of creation and fall. The mores of culture changes with time, while the order of creation is supra-cultural and is valid whatever the time and place. Attempts have been made to localize Paul's prohibition to only the assembly at Ephesus.[35] This simply cannot be illustrated by the NT texts which treat these matters. The following should be kept in mind when encountering such an argument which has become part and parcel of egalitarian attempts at explaining away the Pauline prohibitions.

---

[34] William Hendrickson, *Exposition of the Pastoral Epistles* (Grand Rapids: Baker, 1957), 110.

[35] Spencer's reason for localizing the prohibition to Ephesus is her assumption that a female heretic was teaching false doctrine in that church. Because this woman (or women), Paul's judgment was that the women in Ephesus should learn in silence from the authoritative teachers. This is a rather large assumption since no female teacher is mentioned in the Pastorals and the one passage to which she alludes (2 Tim 3:5-7) refers to women being led astray by male false teachers! (Spencer, 216). For this "localizing" view, see also Scanzoni and Hardesty, 37. Recent writers who have treated the passage in a similar manner are Fee, 1990; Payne, 2008; and Westfall, 2016.

Paul goes out of his way to counter any suspicion that his teaching is of merely local or temporary significance. He grounds His regulations in basic theological affirmations which are quite independent of time and place. ... Whatever our opinion of Paul's arguments we must recognize that they are not the arguments of a man bowing to expediency. In his own intention his teaching was not a concession to local and temporary circumstances but an enunciation of principles valid for all time and in every place.[36]

Although the interpretation of the problematic clause in 2:15 ("but she shall be saved in childbearing") is not vital to the outcome of this discussion, an interpretation is here offered. This writer prefers the translation, "But she shall be preserved through the bearing of children." This rendering takes the future verb *sothesetai* (σωθήσεται) in the general sense of "deliver" and the noun *teknogonias* (τεχνογονίας) as a description of the entire process of childbearing. This is meant to convey encouragement to women in the natural sphere. This certainly accords well with the Genesis account which announces to Eve that she shall conceive in pain, with Paul adding the assurance that such sorrowful pain will not be unbearable and safe delivery (of the woman) is assured if the conditions are observed.[37]

1 Corinthians 14:33b-35

---

[36] Donald MacLeod, "The Place of Women in the Church," *The Banner of Truth*, No. 81 (June, 1970), 35-36.

[37] For an excellent summary of the interpretations that have been suggested about the meaning of this verse, see Donald Guthrie, *The Pastoral Epistles* (London: The Tyndale Press, 1957), 77-79. Recent writers defending a complementarian view of this passage are Archer, 1982; Baugh, 1992; Bowman, 1992; Culver, 1989; Piper and Grudem, 1991; Kostenberger and Schreiner, 2005. Porter's article (1993) on the interpretation of 2:15 is very valuable.

The second strong prohibition that Paul makes regarding the participation of women in the public ministry of the church relates also to her involvement vocally. This passage states:

> As in all the churches of the saints, let the women keep silent in the churches; for they are not permitted to speak, but let them subject themselves, just as the Law also says. And if they desire to learn anything, let them ask their own husbands at home; for it is improper for a woman to speak in church.

Some have simply rejected this passage as spurious (i.e., vv. 34-35) because of a textual problem involved. Philip Payne has been the most articulate exponent of the textual invalidity of these verses.[38] These two verses are transposed following verse

---

[38] Payne has argued this position often (see the bibliography) and summarizes it in *Man and Woman: One in Christ* (Grand Rapids: Zondervan, 2009), 225-67. Payne has argued convincingly that two dots (called more accurately *distigmai*) that appear often in the margins of Codex Vaticanus indicate that a scribe knew of a variant reading at this point. The two dots appear in the margin of Vaticanus above and left of the beginning of these verses. Payne argues that the scribe knew that they were omitted in the manuscript tradition; hence they are not in the original. The problem with this is two-fold.1. We are not sure that the dots came from the original scribe, since most scholars believe that these dots date from the fifteenth century. 2. Even if the scribe responsible for the *distigmai* was the original scribe of Vaticanus, the most that it proves is that he knew that the verses were transposed after verse 40 – not that they were omitted. The fact remains that no manuscript of the epistle omits these words. For a critique of his text-critical arguments, see Kloha's unpublished dissertation (2006), available online (see bibliography). For another critique of his overall argument, see Thomas R. Schreiner, "A Review of Philip Payne: Man and Woman in Christ" in the *Journal of Biblical Manhood and Womanhood*, (Spring, 2010. Volume XV, Number One): 33-46.

40 in a few manuscripts of the Western family type.[39] However, the vast majority of manuscripts, including early representatives of all the major textual families, include the verses in their normal location.[40] Furthermore, the most telling argument against the exclusion of these verses is that while they are transposed in the few manuscripts cited, no known Greek manuscript omits these verses. This is the most serious fault with Payne's theory. A recent academic article by a female scholar has decisively answered Payne's arguments against the authenticity of these two verses.[41] Therefore, we accept with good authority the genuine antiquity of the verses.

However, the traditional verse division is questionable. Most editions of Greek Testaments begin a new sentence and paragraph in verse 33 with the phrase, "As in all the churches of the saints." That sentence is then coupled with verse 34 to convey the following idea, "As in all the churches of God's holy people, women should be quiet in your church meetings."[42] The thought expressed in verse 33 is a culminating conclusion to what he had said before and needs no statement to complete it, "for God is not a God of confusion but of peace." The customary practice that Paul is referring to is not the custom of God's bringing peace, but the uniform custom of women's silence in all the churches. Another question that has to be answered is this: "Is the silence that Paul invokes

---

[39] D, G, 88, some Old Latin mss and Ambrosiaster and Sedulius-Scotus.

[40] p46, ℵ, A, B, K, ψ, all uncials and cursives, some Old Latin mss, Vulgate, Syriac, Coptic, and Armenian versions.

[41] "A Text Without 1 Corinthians 14.34-35? Not According to the Manuscript Evidence," Jennifer Shack, *Journal of Greco-Roman Christianity and Judaism*, 10 (2014) 90-112.

[42] F. F. Bruce, *The Letters of Paul* (Grand Rapids: Wm. B. Eerdmans Publishing Company, 1965), 113.

referring to tongues?" Occasionally, some writers have taken this view.[43] This interpretation says that the entire chapter has to do with "speaking" in tongues. Since verses 2, 4, 5-6, 11, 13, 18, 23, and 27 all mention "speak" (*laleo* - λαλέω) with "tongue" or "tongues," then when Paul says that women are not permitted to speak, he means that they are not permitted to speak in tongues in the public assembly. However, this attention to the larger context neglects attention to the immediate context. Beginning at verse 29, the discussion concerns prophesying, not tongues-speaking. After issuing the "rules" regulating tongues in verses 26-28, Paul then issues "rules" regulating prophesying in verses 29-38. Therefore, we conclude that whatever the silence means, it is used in some connection with prophesying, not tongues-speaking.

Before we give consideration to what this silence really means, the reason for the prohibition of silence must be noted. Two reasons are mentioned: (1) because of what the "Law" says (v. 34), and (2) because it is "improper." Whenever a New Testament writer refers to the "Law" in citing the Scriptures he may be referring to any section of the Old Testament. Previously in the chapter (14:21) Paul quotes Isaiah 28:11 and says that it is in "the Law." In John 10:34 Jesus quoted from Psalm 82 and said that it was "in your Law." So "the Law" does not always refer to what is called the "Torah," or the first five books of the Old Testament. Paul may very well be referring to the order of creation and order of the fall in Genesis 2 and 3. If he is, then this would be the same reason he appeals when he forbids teaching by women in 1 Timothy 2:12-14. However, he may be referring to the entire thrust of the OT Scriptures as teaching the subordination of women. Either way, the Law says that women are to be silent as a mark of their

---

[43] Lehman Strauss, *Speaking in Tongues* (Philadelphia: Bible Study Time, 1974), 15, 16.

subordination. It does not say it in so many words, but the principle of woman's subordination in creation (referred to earlier in 1 Cor 11:8-9) finds its application in Corinth in women's silence.

The second reason for a woman's silence is that "it is improper for a woman to speak in the church." The word *aischron* (αἰσχρòν) is translated "disgraceful" by the New American Standard Bible in its other two appearances in the NT (1 Cor 11:6 and Eph 5:12). This refers to how others in the church or outside of the church would view a woman's usurping authority over a man. Thus, in this passage Paul gives both a "creation" reason and a "cultural" reason for his prohibition. When one considers Paul's reasons as they relate to today's application, he may have justification in believing that the latter reason could change with a changing culture. However, the appeal to the "law" remains valid as long as the "Law" remains valid. A frequent interpretation of this passage views the women in Corinth as being guilty of "chattering" during the service. Consider Barbara Hampton's explanation, which has been repeated by many authors.

> In the Corinthian church (as in other places, we can infer from v. 33), women were "chattering" (meaning of "speak" in v. 35), interrupting the service with questions, disrupting the decency and order of the worship and teaching. Given … their likely pre-Christian background, their disturbances are not surprising, but nonetheless had to be dealt with.[44]

This interpretation, in effect, localizes Paul's prohibition to the Corinthian situation. It also removes it from any reference to the question of women being pastors, teachers, etc. This

---

[44] Barbara Hampton, "What Did St. Paul Want?," *HIS*, (1973), 12.

interpretation, however, rests on the basic assumption that the "speak" (*lalein* - λαλεῖν) of verse 34 means "chatter." The verb *laleo* (λαλέω) appears 295 times in the New Testament and it is never translated as "chatter."[45] To assume that the confusion characteristic of the Corinthian meetings was due to chattering women is reading far more into the context than is there.

What is the meaning of the silence enjoined on women in this passage? First of all, assuming Paul is consistent with himself, a harmony must be sought that forbids women the authoritative teaching function (as is done in 1 Timothy 2:12-14), but also allows freedom for a woman to pray and prophesy in the assembly. Paul assumes that women do this (1 Tim 2:9; 1 Cor 11:5). Whatever "prophesying" entails, it is not regarded as the same function as teaching, else the apostle involves himself in an irreconcilable contradiction. In other words, this prohibition against speaking is not absolute. When "speaking" is defined as authoritative teaching, it is absolute, but it does not mean absolute silence in all things. The passage does mean absolute abstention from any activity that exercises authority over man. Evidently praying and prophesying do not involve the same type of authority. Thus the apostle's statement here is consistent with 1 Timothy 2:12-14 in forbidding ministry that exercises authority over men. However, although verses 34-35 certainly forbid what Paul forbids elsewhere, in the context of the chapter they have further application. James Hurley has offered an interpretation which is consistent with the entire epistle and the chapter itself.

> Verse 29 outlines principles to govern the exercise of the prophetic gifts of the Spirit. Two or three prophets are to speak and the

[45] J. B. Smith, *Greek-English Concordance* (Scottsdale, Pa.: Herald Press, 1955), 212. Smith's exhaustive research reveals that the word is translated in the KJV as "speak" 246 times, "say" 15 times, "tell" 12 times, "talk" 12 times, "preach" 6 times, and "utter" 4 times. See also BDAG, 582-83.

others are to pass judgment. Verses 30-33a elaborate upon the manner in which the prophets are to speak: They are to maintain order, being silent when another is given a message. Verse 33b-35 deal with a particular problem which had arisen with regard to the second half of Paul's outline in v. 29, the judging of the prophets. Paul required that the others judge the prophets, discussing and evaluating their messages to explore the meaning and to see that they were not false to the gospel. Women were among the prophets and it would seem the women entered into the judgment of the prophets as well, thereby assuming the anomalous role of judging men. It is to this situation that Paul addressed himself as he forbade the women to speak. Paul's wording shows that the antithesis in his mind was not simply that of silence or speaking but rather the subjection to or violation of created authority structure. It is clear from Chapter II that Paul did not understand charismatic prayer or prophecy from women as violations of this order, as these involve no direct authority on the part of the speaker. It would, however, be a violation were women to sit in judgment over men. If we envisage a question period after the prophecies in which the congregation explored and evaluated the messages of the prophets, we have a setting adequate to explain Paul's injunction.[46]

---

[46] James B. Hurley, "Did Paul Require Veils or the Silence of Women? A Consideration of I Cor. 11:2-16 and I Cor. 14:33b-36," *Westminster Theological Journal*, Vol. XXXV, No. 2, 1973, 217.

With this explanation, verse 35 is not meant to prevent learning, but rather to prevent a wrong exercise of authority. If women discussed with their husbands (most likely at a distance since they may have been separated, as in the synagogues), a disturbance certainly would result. Paul was vitally concerned, however, with the instruction of the women, as was exemplified in 1 Timothy 2:11. Therefore, they were to ask their husbands at home, rather than disturb the service and abuse the authority structure by judging men. Hurley gives an extended paraphrase of 1 Corinthians 14:29, 33a-35 in summary.

> And let two or three prophets speak and let the others judge what they say as true Gospel. Let the women keep silent and not enter into the judgment of the prophets for they are not permitted to participate in the formal judgment of men. Let them rather subject themselves as Genesis also directs. If they have questions about the teaching they should not pose them during the judging of the prophets, nor should they walk across the assembly to their husbands. If they wish to learn more they should ask their husbands at home.[47]

From the exegesis of these two passages, we conclude that Paul limited the authoritative teaching of the church (elders/overseers/pastors) to men. His concern about silence for women is not absolute, but refers to teaching that exercises spiritual authority over men in the assemblies.

Pauline Pronouncements

The two passages in which Paul issues prohibitions

---

[47] Hurley, 220.

regarding women's function in the vocal ministry have been noted. There are two other passages where Paul makes certain pronouncements regarding women that are crucial to the understanding of their role in the church.

These passages are 1 Corinthians 11:2-16 and Galatians 3:28.

1 Corinthians 11:2-16

Now I praise you because you remember me in everything and hold firmly to the traditions, just as I delivered them to you. But I want you to understand that Christ is the head of every man, and the man is the head of a woman, and God is the head of Christ. Every man who has something on his head while praying or prophesying disgraces his head. But every woman who has her head uncovered while praying or prophesying disgraces her head, for she is one and the same as the woman whose head is shaved. For if a woman does not cover her head, let her also have her hair cut off; but if it is disgraceful for a woman to have her hair cut off or her head shaved, let her cover her head. For a man ought not to have his head covered, since he is the image and glory of God; but the woman is the glory of man. For man does not originate from woman, but woman from man; for indeed man was not created for the woman's sake, but woman for the man's sake. Therefore the woman ought to have a symbol of authority on her head, because of the angels.
However, in the Lord, neither is woman independent of man, nor is man independent of woman. For as the woman

originates from the man, so also the man
has his birth through the woman; and all
things originate from God. Judge for
yourselves: is it proper for a woman to pray
to God with her head uncovered? Does not
even nature itself teach you that if a man
has long hair, it is a dishonor to him, but if
a woman has long hair, it is a glory to her?
For her hair is given to her for a covering.
But if one is inclined to be contentious, we
have no other practice, nor have the
churches of God.

First Corinthians 11:2-14:40 deals with order and
disorder in public worship. The first section (11:2-16) deals
with the principle of headship/authority and how it relates to
praying and prophesying. The second section (11:17-34) deals
with the nature of the Lord's Supper and its observance and
abuse. The third section (12:1-14:40) deals with the broader
subject of spiritual gifts – their nature, exercise, and abuse.

It is important to note that the primary concern of the
Apostle in 1 Corinthians 11:2-16 is to expound the divine order
and authority that is inherent in the structure of the universe.
His primary purpose is not to teach about "head-coverings,"
although the matter certainly relates to his primary purpose.
His concern is how believers relate to God-ordained authority.
Too often this and other chapters of the New Testament are
conveniently set aside as "cultural" with no application for
today.   In disregarding cultural items, oftentimes the
permanent eternal principle is lost. In this passage Paul deals
with permanent principles, as he does in 1 Corinthians 14:34
and 1 Timothy 2:13-14.   Also, the passage itself contains
indications that Paul is not saying that "This is the way I want
it done in Corinth," with the implication that what he says has
no real application in other cultures. He praises them for
"holding firmly to the traditions, just as I delivered them to
you" (v. 2). These traditions are not simply man-made ideas

that can be discarded with changing times. They also had been handed down to Paul. "For I received from the Lord that which I also delivered to you…," was his remark later in the chapter concerning the "tradition" of the Lord's Supper (1 Cor 11:23). Such "traditions," some of which are discussed in verses 2-16, are to be taken seriously. Furthermore, within the passage Paul appeals to the universal practice of the church for any in Corinth who wanted to argue that they were being subjected to special, discriminatory treatment. "But if one is inclined to be contentious, we have no other practice, nor have the churches of God" (v. 16).

Paul begins with a clear theological statement of headship. "But I want you to understand that Christ is the head of every man, and the man is the head of the woman, and God is the head of Christ" (v. 3). The figure suggested by "head" is that of superiority of position. In other words, the one who has a "head" is subject in function and position to that head. Although recent egalitarian authors have stressed the meaning of *kefale* (κεφαλή) as "source," Wayne Grudem in a number of writings has traced the meaning of the word in Greek literature and concluded that its primary meaning is "head" in the sense of one higher in function.[48] It should be noted that these three relationships (God/Christ, Christ/man, man/woman) are not identical in every respect. No two correspond in all points. However, in one respect they do correspond. In all three relationships there is a head and one subject to that who acknowledges the head.

To say that God is the head of Christ is not to deny that He is also head of man and head of woman. To say that Christ is head of the man is not to deny that He is also head of the woman. What is intended is that while man has only God and Christ as his head, woman has an additional head, the man. She is not the man's head, nor is she under Christ only as her head. This hierarchy of headship and submission is valid

---

[48] See, e.g., Wayne Grudem, "The meaning of κεφαλή ('Head'): An Evaluation of New Evidence" *JETS* 44 (2001): 25-65.

independent from time or place.

An interesting sidelight of this passage speaks to this question. Someone might ask, "If woman is *subordinate* to man, does that not imply her inherent *inferiority* to man?" Our passage under consideration answers that question negatively. Here we have described a *hierarchy* in which there is subordination of position and function, not an *inferiority* of person. This point acknowledges, of course, the distinction between deity and humanity. God is said to be the "head" of Christ. Does that mean that the Son is somehow essentially inferior to the Father, i.e., someone less than fully God? Christian theology recognizes the equality of the Father and the Son in their essence, yet discerns some subordination of the Son to the Father in His function as the mediatorial redeemer.

> On this subject the Nicene doctrine includes ... the principle of the subordination of the Son to the Father, and of the Spirit to the Father and the Son. But this subordination does not imply inferiority. For as the same divine essence with all its infinite perfections is common to the Father, Son, and Spirit, there can be no inferiority of one person to the other in the Trinity. The subordination intended is only that which concerns the mode of subsistence and operation, implied in the Scriptural facts that the Son is of the Father, and the Spirit is of the Father and the Son, and that the Father operates through the Son, and the Father and Son through the Spirit.[49]

---

[49] Charles Hodge, *Systematic Theology* (Grand Rapids: Wm. B. Eerdmans Publishing Company, 1970) I, 460-61.

This is what Jesus meant when Jesus said in the same book, "My Father is greater than I," and "I and my Father are one" (John 14:28; 10:30). There is a very real sense that Jesus is equal to His Father in essence as God, yet also is subordinate in His function as Redeemer (see Philippians 2:5-11). In the same way, the subordination of woman to man does not imply her essential inferiority to him. Both are made in the image of God (Gen 1:27), and the affirmation of the gospel is that "there is no male and female" in Christ (Gal 3:28). However, that does not rule out a subordination of the woman to the man in her function as woman in God's order for her.[50]

Verses 4-7 discuss how this matter of headship and authority is to be manifested in the praying and prophesying ministries of the church. A man who "has something on his head" (*kata kephales echon* - κατὰ κεφαλῆς ἔχων) while he is praying or prophesying "disgraces his head" (*kataischune ten kephalen autou* - καταισχύνει τὴν κεφαλὴν αὐτοῦ). Paul gives the reason why this is so in verse 7, "For a man ought not to have his head covered, since he is the image and glory of God... ." Man should not have a sign indicating the dominion of a man over him. However, for the woman the warning is different in 11:5, "But every woman who has her head uncovered while praying or prophesying, disgraces her head...." Since in the context the woman is to be subordinate to her head, she is to

---

[50] James Olthuis destroys only a "straw-man" when he writes, "If we conclude from this passage that man is by nature (ontically) superior to women, we must likewise conclude that Christ is subordinate by nature to God. The church has denied the second conclusion; it is time she emphatically rejects the first." *I Pledge You My Troth* (New York: Harper and Row Publishers, 1975), 137. Olthuis does not refer to anyone who holds such a view. That man is ontically superior to woman is not necessitated in a correct view of the passage. Olthuis fails to discern the distinction between subordination of function and subordination of nature.

have some "covering" on her head to symbolize her subordination.[51]

At this point some consideration must be given to what is meant by the reference to women praying and prophesying in 1 Corinthians 11:5. Some interpreters have concluded that this reference contradicts the Pauline prohibitions in 1 Timothy 2:12 and 1 Corinthians 14:34.[52] Others have said that this reference is evidence that women exercised the ministry of preaching along with men in the early church.[53] Assuming that Paul does not contradict himself and the texts are not later interpolations, are we correct in viewing 1 Timothy 2:12 and 1 Corinthians 14:34 as forbidding the teaching authority of an elder to women? George Knight asks us to consider the following.

> But clearly, 1 Cor. 14 and 1 Tim. 2 are the
> didactic passages which self-consciously deal

---

[51] The much-debated question of the "head-covering" cannot be adequately discussed without an extensive examination of the various views – a discussion that is not within the scope of this book. The author favors the position that the covering is the "hair" given to a woman and not an object placed on her head. See W.J. Martin, "1 Corinthians 11:2-16: An Interpretation," in *Apostolic History and the Gospel*, ed. W.W. Gasque and Ralph Martin (Grand rapids: Eerdmans Publishing Co., 1970), 231-41. For the view that it is a separate covering, see Leroy Birney, *The Role of Women in the NT Church* (Christian Brethren Research Fellowship, 1971). For the view that the "covering" refers to a woman's hair being up or down, see Hurley, 205ff.

[52] Krister Stendahl, *The Bible and the Role of Women* (Philadelphia: Fortress Press, 966), 35.

[53] Jewett, 170; Scanzoni and Hardesty, 61; Irene Robbins, "St. Paul and the Ministry of Women," *Expository Times*, XLIV, No. 4 (January 1935), 186.

with the subject and 1 Cor. 11 only mentions an aspect incidentally. This consideration demands that the former two be considered the foundational passages and then that 1 Cor. 11 with its incidental reference be integrated with them and not vice-versa. It also is appropriate to presume that the great apostle Paul does not contradict himself within the same letter and only a few chapters apart.[54]

Several solutions have been proposed that seek to maintain a consistent position throughout the New Testament. First, some have attempted to avoid the problem by saying that the prophesying was not done in the church, so this is not a contradiction of 1 Corinthians 14 and 1 Timothy 2.[55] However, in view of the context of the chapter and book, this does not seem to be the case.

Second, some have said that Paul only mentions the activity of prophesying in 11:5 as an activity that is going on in the church. He simply mentions it without approving it or disproving it (unless it is done without the covering). When Paul returns to the issue in chapter 14:29ff, he forbids it in the church.[56] Although this is possible, it does not seem to fit Paul's procedure in dealing with matters that he knows are

---

[54] George W. Knight, III, *The Role Relation of Man and Woman and the Teaching/Ruling Functions in the Church* (St. Louis: printed by author, 1975), 9-10.

[55] Charles Hodge, *An Exposition of the First Epistle to the Corinthians* (Grand Rapids: Wm. B. Eerdmans Publishing Co., 1953); and R.C. H. Lenski, *St. Paul's First and Second Epistles to the Corinthians* (Minneapolis: Augsburg Publishing House, 1963), 437.

[56] A. Robertson and A. Plummer, *I Corinthians* (Edinburgh: T. Clark, 1914), 324. Also R. St. John Parry, *The First Epistle of Paul the Apostle to the Corinthians* (Cambridge: University Press, 1926), 113.

wrong.

Third, one writer asserts that Paul was actually criticizing the case of a woman prophesying.

> The man cannot cover his head when he engages in an authoritative function. For a woman to engage in prayer or prophesy would place her in the same position as man. That is, she would be forced to exercise headship and thus uncover her head. An uncovering of her head accompanies her act of prayer and prophecy.[57]

Because she must uncover her head to perform an authoritative function, then this function must be wrong. However, this interpretation depends on a translation of the dative in verse 5, "Every woman praying or prophesying, by means of the unveiling of the head, dishonors her head."[58] Although this translation is possible, and the interpretation has much to commend it, there is a better solution consistent with all of Scripture.

Fourth, the action of prophesying in 11:5 should be viewed as being in a different category from what is forbidden in 1 Corinthians 14 and 1 Timothy 2. The gifts of prophecy and teaching are distinct gifts (1 Cor 12:29). The authoritative speaking, teaching, and ruling function is denied to women. By the fact of its recognition here, the function of prophecy is allowed to women. What then is this prophecy and how does it differ from teaching?

---

[57] Noel Weeks, "Of Silence and Head Covering," *Westminster Theological Journal*, Vol. XXV, No. 1: 26.

[58] Weeks, 26.

The New Testament speaks of this activity (prophecy) as a result of God's Spirit acting in and through a person to produce that which is God's revelation and that it is regarded therefore as intrinsically different from and distinguished from what the New Testament means by teaching or preaching.[59]

Evidently, the apostle did not view prophecy as being the same as teaching, because prophecy does not involve the same type of teaching-authority that is to be handled by men. This solution preserves the didactic element of 1 Corinthians 14 and 1 Timothy 2 and harmonizes all the passages. It is in accord with the function of female prophets both in the Old and New Testaments.[60] They give a message from God, but do not occupy the "settled" teaching/ruling ministries of elder/overseers. "Whatever women functioning as prophets entailed, it does not follow that women should serve as elders or overseers of God's flock."[61] *Therefore, the Apostle forbade the teaching function to women, but he recognized the prophetic function of women when the prophetic gift was active as part of the foundational character of the apostolic church.* This permission of "prophetesses" was thus appropriate in the First Century era when God was

---

[59] Knight, 10.

[60] See Exo 15:20; Num 12:1, 2; Jdgs 4:4-7; 2 Kgs 23:13-20 and Acts 21:9.

[61] Thomas Schreiner, "Women in Ministry: Another Complementarian Perspective" in *Two Views on Women in Ministry.* Ed. James Beck, 2nd edition (Grand Rapids: Zondervan, 2005). Schreiner ably defends the complementarian view in this chapter and in other articles (see bibliography).

still speaking directly to His servants in prophetic utterances.[62]

When New Testament writers command the woman to be subordinate, they never do so on a purely arbitrary basis. Such is also the case in this passage. The reason that Paul gives for the woman's subordinate attitude is, again, the order of creation. A literal translation of verses 8-9 would read,

> For man is not out of woman, but woman is out of man; for indeed man was not created for the woman, but woman (was created) for the man.

The obvious reference is again to Genesis 2:20-23. The familiar comment of Adam was "...she shall be called Woman (*ishah* אִשָּׁה), because she was taken out of a Man (*ish* אִישׁ)" (v. 23). This thought is similar to that expressed in 1 Timothy 2:13. However, that verse emphasized the order of creation. These verses emphasize not only the order of creation, but the dependence of the woman on the man as her ground of being. "It is to underscore man's dominion that Paul introduced the fact that the woman was created to have a relation to the man

---

[62] The question as to how all this relates to the ministry of women today depends whether or not the "charismatic" sign gifts have ceased. For a convincing argument that the "sign-gifts" have ceased see the following: Benjamin B. Warfield, *Counterfeit Miracles* (London: Banner of Truth Trust, 1972), 1-33; Walter J. Chantry, *Signs of the Apostles* (Edinburgh: Banner of Truth Trust, 1973), 16-40; and John MacArthur, *Strange Fire: The Danger of Offending the Holy Spirit with Counterfeit Worship* (Nashville: Thomas Nelson, 2013). Recently some have espoused the idea that God can give a revelatory prophecy that is not intended to be part of scriptural revelation, and thus that the prophecy could even be untrue. The response to this is that the idea of a divinely inspired but fallible prophecy is simply not entertained in the New Testament.

rather than vice versa."[63] This is not to deny the fact that she is fully human and is also in the image of God. The fact that in verse 7 Paul says that man is "the image and glory of God," while "women is the glory of man" is not denying that she also is in the image of God. Paul doesn't deny that, but is defining her relationship to man, not God, in the context of the discussion.

Lest someone misunderstand his meaning and pervert his teaching into the conclusion of woman's inherent inferiority, Paul adds in verses 11-12:

> However, in the Lord, neither is woman independent of man, nor is man independent of woman. For as the woman originates from the man, so also the man has his birth through the woman; and all things originate from God.

Paul refers to the natural dependence of a man on a woman in every birth to illustrate the fact that there is also a mutual dependence of one on the other. Man does not simply exist "without" (*choris* - χωρὶς) the woman, or vice versa. God made them both that they might "cleave together" and be "one flesh" (Gen 2:24). Diversity in unity is His purpose. Man is not to think of himself as self-sufficient, but is to recognize that there is to be a natural submission "in the Lord," i.e., all believers are to "submit one to another" (Eph 5:21). That such a mutual submission of all the members of Christ is not inconsistent within a structure of authority is evident from a statement made by Peter. Within a context in which he emphasizes the submissiveness of wives to husbands, he reminds the husbands:

---

[63] Hurley, 206.

> You husbands in the same way, live with
> your wives in an understanding way, as
> with someone weaker, since she is a
> woman; and show her honor as a fellow
> heir of the grace of life, so that your prayers
> will not be hindered (1 Pet 3:7).

To say that Paul in 1 Corinthians 11:11-12 is manifesting an "uneasy conscience" is to charge him with the worst sort of ambivalence. Paul is not wrestling with a "tension in his thought."[64] He is not concerned that he may be mistaken in this matter. His concern is that others may not make the mistake of emphasizing the *subordination responsibility* to the total detriment of the *mutual respect responsibility*. That modern writers cannot reconcile mutual submission with an overall context of authority structure is due to their inability to comprehend; not to ambivalence on the part of the apostles. To posit such a dialectic in Paul's thought is to destroy his authority as an apostle to teach and write as the Spirit of God revealed to him the mind of God.

> If anyone thinks he is a prophet or spiritual,
> let him recognize that the things which I
> write to you are the Lord's commandment.
> But if anyone does not recognize this, he is
> not recognized (1 Cor 14:37-38).

1 Cor 11:2-16 is consistent with the other passages discussed (1 Tim 2:12-14; 1 Cor 14:34) in recognizing an authority structure with functions of headship and submission. Although the passage does not contain a prohibition to women's teaching, it further amplifies the reason for that prohibition and grounds it once again in the order of creation.

---

[64] Scanzoni and Hardesty, 28, 213.

Galatians 3:28

The "Women's Liberation" or "Feminist" movement of the sixties and seventies had been primarily a secular thrust. However, there are a number of religious authors, often bearing often the label "evangelical," who eventually offered various religious and Biblical arguments for the equality of the sexes. These writers are referred to as "Christian Feminists." It is their conviction that the New Testament contains clear examples of a "new" relationship in Christ between the sexes. They oppose a "sexual hierarchy" or "divine chain of command," which is inconsistent with egalitarianism. One of the texts on which they base their ideas is Galatians 3:28: "There is neither Jew nor Greek, there is neither slave nor free man, there is neither male nor female; for you are all one in Christ Jesus." It is the purpose of this section to explore the "Christian Feminist" use of this text, to analyze the text with a grammatical-contextual method, and to seek its interpretation as it relates to the unity of male and female "in Christ Jesus."

The Issue Involved

Throughout the history of "Christian Feminist" literature, Galatians 3:28 has been considered the *locus classicus* for a New Testament understanding of male-female relations. The first woman to be ordained in America was Antoinette Brown, a graduate of Oberlin College. In 1853 she was ordained in the Congregational Church of South Butler, New York. The preacher for the service was Luther Lee, a founder of the Wesleyan Methodist Church. Lee's sermon, entitled "Women's Right to Preach the Gospel," was based on Galatians 3:28.[65]

---

[65] Donald W. and Lucille Sider Dayton "Women as Preachers - Evangelical Precedents," *Christianity Today* (May 23, 1975) 5.

Among contemporary writers on this subject, Galatians 3:28 has been viewed as the key text in an argument for Christian "egalitarianism." The late Krister Stendahl of Harvard Divinity School writes:

> In the same way the fundamental view determined by the order of creation found in the Haustefeln (Ephesians 5:22-33) and I Corinthians 11 and 14 is broken through in the well-known passage in Galatians. It should be noted that this statement is directed against what we call the order of creation, and consequently it creates a tension with those Biblical passages – Pauline and non-Pauline – by which this order of creation maintains its place in the fundamental view of the New Testament concerning the subordination of women. There can be no doubt that Paul did everything in his power to apply this principle in the actual life of his congregation.[66]

Letha Scanzoni and Nancy Hardesty have clearly perceived the importance of Galatians 3:28. After discussing the various passages which restrict the participation of women in public church activities, they note:

> (Each) passage seems directed to a particular situation rather than at stating a general principle. Of all the passages concerning women in the New Testament, only Galatians 3:28 is in a doctrinal setting; the remainder are all concerned with practical matters. Paul in Galatians was

---

[66] Stendahl, 31-33. See also Westfall, 166-72.

serious; he did not get carried away with rhetoric; his words are intentional. The last phrase, *arsen kai thelu*, uses the technical terms which parallel Genesis 1:27 as quoted by Jesus in Matthew 19:40. Paul here is not denying certain distinctions between groups. None of the apostles advocated the immediate overthrow of cultural custom. Yet they did not shy away from the radical cutting edge of the gospel which would gradually undermine society's repressive policies and restore God's intended harmony. Both Greeks and Jews were accepted by Christianity on an equal footing. Slaves and free men became brothers. Men and women worked side-by-side in spreading the gospel. There were no second-class citizens in Christ's church.[67]

One of the most able theological affirmations of women's full equality with man was presented by Paul King Jewett in *Man as Male and Female.* In rejecting the "Hierarchical view of the Man/Woman relationship in favor of one of partnership," Jewett concludes his argument with a thorough treatment of Galatians 3:28, which he calls "The Magna Carta of Humanity."[68] Jewett believed that Paul is referring to Genesis 1:27 by the use of the phrase "male and female" (*arsen kai thelu* - ἄρσεν καὶ θῆλυ). Jewett saw a tension between the two creation narratives. Chapter one of Genesis teaches full equality with its expression of both male and female being made in the image of God. Chapter two of Genesis, however, is appealed to by Paul sometimes to teach subordination of the

---

[67] Scanzoni and Hardesty, 71-72.

[68] Jewett, 129.

woman (e.g. 1 Tim 2:12), because of its expression of male-female order in creation.

> We have noted that the apostle never appeals to the first creation narrative when speaking of the woman's submission to the man. However, in Galatians 3:28, when speaking of her equality with the man, he does allude to the narrative.[69]

Jewett then shows how each of these three divisions: race (Jew and Greek), class (slave and free), and sex (male and female), have no longer have a place in Christ. The apostle himself exemplified what he taught by his own life.

> And the affirmation that in Christ there is no male and female (Gal.3:28) was, for the apostle, not merely a matter of theory. He acted out this truth in a most remarkable way, for a former rabbi. In fact, the apostle, who has been maligned as a misogynist, greets by name no less than seven Christian women in Romans 16 – a cover letter carried by Phoebe, a woman whom he calls his sister and warmly commends as a servant of the church at Cenchreae (16:1-2). Women evidently played a prominent part in the Philippian Church, not only at its inception, but also as it grew and developed. Two of them are mentioned by name, Euodia and Syntyche, whom Paul calls his "fellow workers, who struggled together with me (συναθλέω) in

---

[69] Jewett., 142.

the spreading of the gospel."[70]

Jewett believes that the Bible presents a "dialectic" in its treatment of women. The repressive attitude of the Old Testament and Judaism is supposedly set over against the egalitarian attitude of Jesus. Jewett believes this dialectic is focused more sharply in Paul, "the former rabbi who became the apostle of Christian liberty. It was he who spoke the most decisive word; both in favor of woman's subjection (1 Cor 11) and in favor of woman's liberation (Gal 3)."[71]

> To understand his thought about the relation of the woman to the man, one must appreciate that he was both a Jew and a Christian. He was a rabbi of impeccable erudition who had become an ardent disciple of Jesus Christ. And his thinking about women – their place in life generally and in the church specifically – reflects both his Jewish and his Christian experience. The traditional teaching of Judaism and the revolutionary new approach implied in the teaching of Jesus contributed, each in its own way, to the apostle's thinking about the relationship of the sexes. So far as he thought in terms of his Jewish background, he thought of woman as subordinate to the man for whose sake she was created (1 Cor 11:9). But so far as he thought in terms of the new insight he had gained through the revelation of God in Christ, he thought of the woman as equal to the man in all things, the two having been made one in Christ in who there is neither male nor female (Gal 3:28).

---

[70] Jewett, 145-47.

[71] Jewett, 86.

Analysis of the Text

The importance that is attached to Galatians 3:28 by Christian Egalitarians is obvious from the foregoing quotations. Are they correct in their interpretation and application of this verse? In answering that question we will need to first analyze and exegete the meaning of the text in its context.

In his epistle to the Galatians Paul is dealing with a problem that had been introduced into the churches and in effect "perverted the gospel of Christ" (1:7). This problem was a doctrinal heresy. The teaching was a denial of the doctrine of justification by grace through faith, which was preached by Paul and which the Galatians had believed and received. It has been labeled as "Judaizing," or "Galatianism," or sometimes simply "legalism."

In chapter three, verses 1-5, the Apostle appeals to their Christian experience as indicative that it was through faith, not works that spiritual blessing was received. Next, Paul begins to cite more Old Testament Scriptural examples as evidence that even before the law was given, faith was the means of acceptance with God. Abraham's faith is the classic example of this (vv. 6-9). The Old Testament itself declares that "the just shall live <u>by faith</u>" (v. 11). Because of man's inability to keep it, the law can only curse – curse from which Christ has redeemed us (vv. 10-13). On the other hand, the promise to Abraham received by faith is a <u>blessing</u>! (v. 14). Further, since a covenant (*diatheke* - διαθήκη) is not annulled by later additions, the law, which comes 430 years later, does not annul the promise of faith given to Abraham (3:15-18). The purpose of the law is to show men their sins and to shut them up so they could have no hope, so that they would believe in Christ. Having accomplished that purpose, the law is through as a system (3:19-25).

In 3:26-28 Paul's theme is the unity of all believers in Christ. "For you are all sons of God through faith in Christ Jesus" (3:26). He then refers to the Christian initiation ceremony (baptism) and employs a clothing analogy in that when "you were baptized into Christ, you put on (or "clothed yourselves with") Christ" (3:27). Then Paul makes his statement with which we are most concerned: "There is neither Jew nor Greek, there is neither slave nor free man, there is neither male nor female; for you are all one in Christ Jesus" (3:28).

The context of the book and the chapter and the paragraph points to the fact that Paul is preeminently concerned with the vertical relationship between a believer and God. By faith in Christ Jesus "all" (Jew, Greek, slave, freeman, male, female) are children of God. The horizontal relationships between a Jew and Greek, between a slave and a free man, and between a male and a female are not here in the apostle's immediate view. Even Jewett, who argues form this verse for egalitarianism, admits that this vertical dimension is what is uppermost in the apostle's thought in Galatians 3.

> Undoubtedly, as we have noted above, in all three of these parts – Jew/Greek, bond/free/ male/female – the apostle thinks preeminently *coram Deo*, that is, in terms of the Man-to-God relationship rather than in terms of the Man-to-Man relationship.[72]

Although Jewett sees more than this, he affirms that the context shows that man's spiritual relationship to God is the theme, not man's social relationship with man. The third clause of the verse is the one most pertinent to our study. It should be noted that each of these first three clauses could count for the entire human population. Everyone is either Jew or Gentile. Everyone is either a slave or a free person. Everyone is either a male or female. The area of emphasis in speaking of the whole world is what is in the apostle's mind, and the area of emphasis here is sex.

While the first two clauses employed the *ouk* ... *oude*

---

[72] Jewett, 144.

(οὐκ ... οὐδὲ) / "neither...nor" construction, the *oude* (οὐδὲ) is absent in the third clause and we read *ouk eni arsen kai thelu* (οὐκ ἔνι ἄρσεν καὶ θῆλυ) .... Special notice is taken of this by Jewett:

> Most versions, for the sake of symmetry, retain the "neither-nor" of the series and render the Greek in this text: "neither male nor female," reflecting the language of Genesis 1:27. Furthermore, the words he uses (ἄρσεν καὶ θῆλυ) are those used in the Septuagint translation of this passage. In contrast, therefore, to his exclusive appeal to the second creation narrative when speaking of the woman's subordination to the man, here the apostle clearly has in mind the first creation narrative.[73]

Paul does not use the general term *anthropos* (ἄνθρωπος) meaning "person" but the word *aner* (ἀνήρ) which emphasizes "maleness" - a word that is used only nine times in the New Testament (Matt 19:4; Mark 10:6; Luke 2:23; Rom 1:27 (3); Gal 3:28; Rev 12:5, 13). Neither does he use the more familiar *gune* ("woman, wife"), but *thelu* (θῆλυ) – an adjective used as a noun translated "female" - which is used only five times in the NT (Matt 19:4; Mark 10:6; Rom 1:26, 27; and Gal 3:28). In two of these occurrences, specific reference is made to Adam and Eve. Such terminology indicates that Paul is probably making a conscious reference to Genesis 1:27.

The final clause, "for you are all one in Christ Jesus" is very important. It shows the sphere in which the unity is found. It belongs to those "in Christ Jesus," or, "those who have been incorporated into Christ by faith in him." Nothing is said of those outside of Christ.

---

[73] Jewett, 142.

Interpretation

The interpretation and application of Galatians 3:28 which is so central to the argument for egalitarianism is summarized by Virginia Mollenkott in her introduction to *Man as Male and Female*.

> To be consistent, any church which insists on keeping women in a first-century relationship to men must also insist upon the reinstitution of slavery as it existed in the first century. New Testament remarks to slaves were intended to comfort and instruct them in a situation which could not be changed overnight, while New Testament remarks about female subordination were intended to comfort and instruct women in a situation which could not be changed overnight, while New Testament principles of love and mutual respect were intended ultimately to destroy all subordination of one half of the human race to the other. Any church or individual who can make cultural distinctions in connection with slavery must in all honesty make similar distinctions about the relationship between men and women as pictured in the New Testament. The liberating vision of Galatians 3:28, not the stultifying first-century actuality, is the ideal to implement.[74]

Is this a correct interpretation and application of Paul's

---

[74] Virginia Mollenkott, Foreword to *Man as Male and Female*, by Paul Jewett (Grand Rapids: Eerdmans Publishing Co., 1975) 11-12.

statement? Let us look first at what the verse does not mean and then look briefly at what it does mean.

Galatians 3:28 does not teach that in Christ, the ordinance of creation, whereby Man is male and female, is done away. The "androgynous ideal," echoing the ancient Greek myth of the Androgyne (a man-woman being) is not in Paul's thought. The writer knows of no evangelicals who would affirm this as the meaning of Galatians 3:28. Mollenkott's recent works, however, seem to be headed in that direction. See the bibliography.

Furthermore, Paul is not abolishing the hierarchical structure of male/female relationship. That he is doing such in this verse is strongly affirmed by Stendahl, Scanzoni and Hardesty, Jewett, Mollenkott and other evangelical authors. The New Testament texts which teach such a hierarchy are 1 Cor 11:2-16: Eph 5:22-33; Col 3:18-19; Tit 2:15; 1 Pet 3:1ff; 1 Cor 14:33-35; and 1 Tim 2:11-15. Jewett himself sums up the teaching of these texts as they relate to woman's subordination.

> The woman is subject to the man because the man, as created first, is directly in the image and glory of God, whereas the woman, created after the man and for him, is the glory of the man. Because of her lesser endowment (presumably) she was deceived by the tempter when the man was not. Therefore she should never aspire to teach the man, but always learn from him in subjection and quiet humility. Specifically, this means that Christian women are not permitted to speak in the Church; in fact it would be shameful were they to do so. Therefore let them study a becoming silence.[75]

---

[75] Jewett, 61, who updates his argument in *The Ordination of Women* (1980). See also Payne and Westfall for a similar approach.

However, Jewett rejects the argument of female subordination as being incompatible with "the analogy of faith," i.e. the fundamental teaching of both the Old and New Testaments of the equality of male and female.[76] This analogy is based on (1) the biblical narrative of Man's creation as teaching partnership, not subordination; (2) the examples of Jesus' attitude to women in the Gospels; and (3) Paul's fundamental statement in Galatians 3:28.

Jewett believes that Paul in the "hierarchy" passages grounds his argument in the order of creation found in Genesis 2. However, Genesis 1 shows that both male and female were created in the image of God, implying equality. This supposed "tension" (or should we say "contradiction") between Genesis 1 and 2 creates quite a problem when one discusses the whole meaning of inspiration and inerrancy. Was Paul "inspired" by God when he appealed to Genesis 2 account in 1 Timothy 2:11-15 as reason for forbidding the teaching ministry to women? Or was Paul reflecting his rabbinical training? Jewett opts for the latter.[77] The serious consequences of such a conclusion cannot be emphasized enough. How can we distinguish when Paul wrote as "Saul the Rabbi" and when he wrote as "Paul the Christian?" Was he inspired when he taught that which agrees with <u>our</u> conception of social relationships? Was he just reflecting his rabbinical antifeminism when he taught that which disagrees with <u>our</u> conception of what male-female relationships should be? Such an attitude raises grave questions about the nature of Scripture.

Furthermore, if Paul's "hierarchy" passages contradict the "analogy of faith", could not that argument be reversed? Could not the "analogy of faith" be contained in Genesis 2 and the New Testament passages cited above? Certainly such a

---

[76] Jewett, 134.

[77] Jewett, 112.

doctrinal statement as 1 Corinthians 11:2 cannot be dismissed as only referring to a cultural situation. "But I would have you to know, that the head of every man is Christ; and the head of every woman is the man; and the head of Christ is God." The analogy of faith is not the first-century attitude of Judaism to women, but these clear statements of a hierarchical relationship grounded in the order of creation. Therefore, such statements as Genesis 1:27 and Galatians 3:28 must be interpreted so as not to contradict the analogy of faith so clearly expressed in these passages.

There remains one more argument of the "Christian feminists" so clearly expressed by Mollenkott in her quotation cited in footnote 74. The argument is that if Paul's liberating vision of "no slave or free" in Christ eventually resulted in the abolition of slavery, should not his vision of "no male and female" in Christ eventually result in the abolition of female subordination to man? Paul recognized that he could not change a situation overnight. However, as the gospel penetrated lives and minds, the structures of society were altered. If this happened with slavery why have we forbidden it to happen with female subordination? In other words, Galatians 3:28 is the ideal – why do we forbid ourselves to follow that ideal? This argument sounds very convincing on the surface. However, it contains one fatal flaw. Whenever New Testament writers gave instructions to slaves to obey their masters, they never grounded such obedience in a creation ordinance (Eph 6:5-9; Col 3:22; 1 Tim 6:1; Tit 2:9-10; 1 Pet 2:18). Rather the motive expressed was one of submission to authority for testimony's sake. The slave/master relationship was not a creation ordinance, but was a result of man's inhumanity to man. Paul's letter to Philemon shows that a believing master should be able to see the basic injustice of such a system. However, Paul's instructions to women to be in subjection to men in worship and family situations were grounded in the order of creation, not in a first-century cultural situation. Cultural situations often should be changed, creation ordinances are not to be treated so lightly.

What is Paul saying in Galatians 3:28? Without contradicting the analogy of faith he is affirming the true equality of male and female in Christ before God (*coram deo*). The context of Galatians 3 points in that direction. Any applications of the text in social realms must not contradict teaching elsewhere in the New Testament. Paul also is speaking to the unscriptural attitudes of "Judaism" towards women. Rabbinic teaching forbade women to hear the Word on the same basis as the man, to participate in the temple worship with men (e.g., "Court of Women"), to act as witnesses in court, to speak to men in public, and other harsh situations. Paul's answer to this overly restrictive attitude is that both male and female partake of the new birth, the forgiveness of sins, the Holy Spirit, the "sonship," and the heirship of all those who are in Christ. Both Paul's and Jesus' examples in their ministries illustrate this loving attitude. However, neither Jesus nor Paul contradicted the analogy of faith in teaching a partnership in marriage, or an authoritative female teaching function on the part of women.

Within the context of Galatians 3 we find an example of how this new equality was to be exemplified in this church. Whereas the sign of covenant membership before Christ (circumcision) was limited to males only, now all the children of God by faith in Christ Jesus (male and female) share the sign of the new covenant community – baptism (3:27). Within the context of the Old Testament theocracy, Gentiles, slaves and women were denied the privilege of circumcision. Male proselytes, however, did receive this sign. Paul asserts that all who have faith in Christ are Abraham's seed and are heirs of the promise. Gentiles and slaves, whether male or female, are a unity in Christ. The outward expression of that unity is the privilege accorded to each one – baptism.

Conclusion on Paul and Women

An objective evaluation of Paul's statements about the function of women in God's order reveals Paul to be neither a "chauvinist" nor a "feminist," in the modern meaning of those terms. He was neither a woman-hater (misogynist) nor an unqualified egalitarian. Paul affirmed the spiritual equality of all believers in Christ – this equality included females as well as males. He nowhere taught an essential inferiority of one sex to the other. Paul did see a difference in function for the sexes. He discerned a divine hierarchy in which woman was to function in subordination to the man. As it relates to the ministry of the word, this subordination is illustrated in the teaching function of the church being limited to the male. That teaching function resides with the elder/bishop. For women to authoritatively teach men would be an abuse of authority – women are not to exercise authority over men. This authority structure is not simply the reflection of first-century Jewish culture, but is rooted in the order of creation and the fall. It is, therefore, a permanently valid principle to be applied in all cultures at all times.

WHAT ARE PROPHETESSES,

DEACONESSES, AND FELLOWORKERS?

The Apostle Paul is well-known for his pronouncements on the "woman-question." By his statements in his epistles, he placed a strong prohibition on the preaching/teaching aspect of women's ministry. However, were his actions wholly consistent with his teachings? There are some who believe that though Paul seemed to be very strict on this matter in his epistles, in his actions he allowed for full participation by women in all forms of ministry.[78] To limit ourselves to Paul's epistolary statements is to miss the whole picture, they say.

> The New Testament's direct advice to women seems encapsulated in 1 Corinthians 14:34 and 1 Timothy 2:11-12. Yet such proof texts focus on only one small corner of a very large picture.... From the beginning (of the Christian church) women participated fully and equally with men.[79]

It is the purpose of this chapter to explore the extent of that equal participation claimed for women in the early church. Particular attention will be given to those passages that have

---

[78] Cf. Constance Parvey, "The Theology and Leadership of Woman in the New Testament," in *Religion and Sexism*, ed. By Rosemary Reuther (New York: Simon and Schuster, 1974), 117-49; Thomas Derek, "The Place of Women in the Church at Philippi," *Expository Times*, vol. 84 (January 1972), 117-20; Dick and Joyce Boldrey, "Women in Paul's Life," *Trinity Studies*, 2 (1972), 1-36.

[79] Scanzoni and Hardesty, 60.

been used to indicate some sort of official function of women in teaching men.

Generally speaking, women were prominent in the life of the church from its very beginning. Women were present in the Upper Room and evidently received the filling of the Holy Spirit in the day of Pentecost (Acts 1:14; 2:3). After the death of Ananias and Sapphira "believers were the more added to the Lord, multitudes both of men and women" (Acts 5:14). They were together with men as the objects of Saul's fierce persecution (Acts 8:3). One of the important meeting places of the church in the early days was the house of Mary, mother of John Mark (Acts 12:12). As the gospel reached out in obedience to the Lord's command, there was a high receptivity to it among women. Women in Samaria received the gospel from Philip and were baptized (Acts 8:12). In Thessalonica, Berea and Athens, prominent women believed the gospel. Some of these were among those who searched the Scriptures diligently (Acts 17:4, 11-12; 17:34). One woman disciple, Tabitha, was held in high esteem by the believers at Joppa, and was greatly mourned at her death (Acts 9:36-42). These and other references to be noted later indicate that women shared in the blessings of the gospel equally with men. But did they share equally with men in the privilege of communicating that gospel? Certain other passages in the Acts and Epistles have been cited as evidence that they did.

Prophecy

In that sermon on the day of Pentecost, Peter declared that the manifestation that the people witnessed was what was spoken of by the prophet Joel in his second chapter, verses 28-32. Part of that prophecy quoted by Peter mentions women.

> And it shall be in the last days, God says, that I will pour forth My Spirit upon all mankind; And your sons and your daughters shall prophesy, and your young

men shall dream dreams; Even upon My
bondslaves both men and women, I will in
those days pour forth My Spirit and they
shall prophesy (Acts 2:17-18).

This passage was used by many of the early feminists of the
nineteenth century as a strong warrant for woman's preaching
of the Gospel.[80] Along with this is the statement later in the
book of Acts regarding Philip and his daughters.

And on the next day we departed and came
to Caesarea; and entering the house of
Philip the evangelist, who was one of the
seven, we stayed with him. Now this man
had four virgin daughters who were
prophetesses (Acts 21:8-9).

It is important to note the brevity of these accounts.
None of the "prophecies" of these four daughters are
mentioned. It is not stated if they ministered in churches or at
home. The statement in Acts 2:17-18 certainly indicates an
even broader extent of the Spirit's effusion in this new age. An
often-overlooked aspect of this passage is its striking parallel

---

[80] Donald W. and Lucille Sider Dayton, "Recovering a Heritage:
Evangelical Feminism," *Post American*, September 1974, 9: "Phoebe
Palmer, a lay evangelist and the major force behind this (holiness)
movement, argued in *The Promise of the Father* (1859) on the basis of
Acts 2 that, as prophesied in Joel 2:28, in the "latter days" the spirit
was to be poured out on daughters as well as sons. The
argument…involved the restoration of a pre-fallen state of equality
as well as a pneumatologically grounded doctrine of the right of
women to preach." It is interesting to note that the male founders
of Oberlin College (Charles Finney), Wheaton College (Charles
Blanchard) and Gordon College (A. J. Gordon) all favored women's
right to preach the gospel. See also Letha Scanzoni, "Feminists and
the Bible," *Christianity Today*, February 2, 1973, 10-15.

with the three "pairs" of Galatians 3:28. Paralleling the statement of "neither Jew nor Greek" is the emphasis of the Spirit's being poured out "on all flesh." Paralleling the statement of "neither slave nor free man" is the emphasis of the Spirit's being poured out on "my bondslaves." Paralleling the statement of "no male and female" is the emphasis of the Spirit's being poured out on "both men and women." A characteristic of the last days is the nondiscriminatory prerogative of the Spirit's being poured out on "whosoever will," despite his ethnic, social, or sexual makeup. However, no mention is made of the prophecies of "my daughters," unless their speaking in tongues can be termed prophesying. Whatever be the case, as has been noted before, prophecy is in another category than teaching. "Since women are forbidden to teach it would seem that the prophet as such was not a teacher."[81] The Acts passage clearly indicates that prophesying is a charismatic ministry (i.e., involving an immediate revelation from God) that was allowed to women in the first century. Since the charismatic gifts were sign gifts during the apostolic period, they were not considered as being in the same category as the settled teaching and ruling ministries of elder/overseers. In considering these texts, it is important to make conclusions only as far as the words go, and not assume things unless they are stated. It is easy to imagine these prophetesses doing many varied things, but we must be content with the brief information that is given.

Women in Philippi

As the gospel penetrated Europe and the predominantly Gentile cities, it is evident that women did play a larger role in church affairs. The first contact for the Gospel in Europe was made in the Roman colony of Philippi. An especially prominent woman is mentioned in connection with

---

[81] R. J. Knowling, "Acts of the Apostles," in *Expositor's Greek Testament* (Grand Rapids: Wm. B. Eerdmans Publishing Company, 1951), II, 445.

the founding of the work there.

> And on the Sabbath day we went outside the gate to a riverside, where we were supposing that there would be a place of prayer; and we sat down and began speaking to the women who had assembled. A woman named Lydia, from the city of Thyatira, a seller of purple fabrics, a worshiper of God, was listening; and the Lord opened her heart to respond to the things spoken by Paul. And when she and her household had been baptized, she urged us, saying, "If you have judged me to be faithful to the Lord, come into my house and stay." And she prevailed upon us. And they went out of the prison and entered the house of Lydia, and when they saw the brethren, they encouraged them and departed (Acts 16:13-15, 40).

It must be assumed that Lydia was either single, or, more probably, widowed. She was a "worshipper of God" (*sebomene ton theon* - σεβομένη τὸν θεόν), a technical phrase "applied to pagans who accepted the ethical monotheism of Judaism and attended the synagogue, but did not obligate themselves to keep the whole Jewish law."[82] There was a great receptivity to Paul's ministry among this group (Acts 13:43; 17:4, 17; 18:7). It was Paul's practice when he visited a new city to attend the synagogue on the first Sabbath to present the Christian message. However, there does not appear to have been a synagogue at Philippi. This was because there was an insufficient number of Jewish males in the city. No number of women could compensate for the absence of even one man

---

[82] Arndt and Gingrich, 753; BDAG, 918.

necessary to complete the required quorum of ten.[83] Therefore, on the Sabbath these women resorted to the "place of prayer" (*proseuchen* - προσευχὴν) to go through the appointed Jewish service for that day. For Paul to teach these women in public was indeed a contravention of accepted Rabbinic behavior (see chapter one for references). Paul here makes practical application of his earlier affirmation in Galatians 3:28. Evidently, the church at Philippi began to meet in Lydia's house after her conversion along with the rest of her household. Again, it is easy to assume that Lydia would lead the congregation in teaching and preaching after Paul's departure. However, no indication of such a procedure is given. As long as the congregation consisted of women and children, this would have been no contradiction of Pauline methodology. However, Paul's ministry at Philippi continued for an indefinite period, and there were other results for the Gospel in that city. We do know, definitely, of one famous male convert – the jailor (Acts 16:25-34).

Also, from the cessation of the "we" passage with Paul's departure from Philippi in Acts 17:1, it must be assumed that the writer of Acts (Luke) stayed with the infant church to teach and guide it until the proper leaders could be prepared to take charge of the work. Luke stayed with the Philippian church until he returned to Jerusalem with Paul on his "Third Missionary Journey" with other brethren (Acts 20:3-6). By that time the needed "overseers" and "deacons" had been appointed, to whom Paul addressed an epistle later in his life (Phil 1:1). Therefore, there is no need to assume that Lydia exercised any authoritative teaching function over men in the church. This is not to demean her tremendously helpful

---

[83] *Pirqe Aboth* iii. 7: "Rabbi Halafta ben Dosu, of the village of Honanya, said, 'when ten people sit together and occupy themselves with the Torah, the Shekhinah abides among them, as it is said, God stands in the congregation of God.'" Evidently women did not qualify as "people."

ministry of assistance, which greatly helped to spread the gospel in that city and also probably constituted her as one of the "fellow workers" in that epistle written later by Paul to Philippi (Phil 4:3).

In that epistle, further evidence is given of the activity of women in the church at Philippi. Two women were so active that their arguing caused Paul to sound one of the few negative notes in the entire epistle.

> I urge Euodia and I urge Syntyche to live in harmony in the Lord. Indeed, true companion, I ask you also to help these women who have shared my struggle in the cause of the gospel, together with Clement also and the rest of my fellow workers, whose names are in the book of life (Phil 4:2-3).

Paul says that when he was there in Philippi, these women "shared my struggle" (*sunethlesan* - συνήθλησάν) in the gospel. Notice of this work is taken by a writer who believes that its significance has not been fully appreciated.

> The verb ἀθλέω meant "to contend" as the athlete strained every muscle to achieve victory in the games. So, with equal dedication these women had contended with all zeal for the victory of the Gospel at Philippi. The Apostle would scarcely have used this strong word if they had merely "assisted with material help" and hospitality, while remaining in the background. The word συνήθλησάν suggests a more active participation in the work of Paul, probably even a vocal declaration of the faith. How far this is true is admittedly a matter of conjecture; what

can be said with certainty, however, is that they contended with the Apostle in the cause of the Gospel and had gained a position of such influence as to make their present conflict a risk to the well-being of the church.[84]

The risk to the well-being of the church, however, may not have been due to the prominence of Euodias and Syntyche, but to the serious nature of their conflict. In a church which Paul praises so much, the struggle of these two women probably stood out in bold contrast. The verb *sunethlesan* (συνήθλησάν) should be translated, "They fought at my side in spreading the gospel."[85] Paul is engaging in some biting irony. He says, in effect, "Quit fighting against each other and fight alongside each other in opposing the real enemy. That's what we did when I was with you in the early days of the work." To assume from this vague word that women preached and taught men in Philippi is to say that Paul practiced in Philippi something that he strongly opposed elsewhere –"hypocrisy," i.e., having one's actions contradict one's teaching (cf. Gal 2:11ff). It is also to employ a poor hermeneutical principle, i.e., assuming from a vague reference an interpretation that contradicts clear teaching on the subject elsewhere.

The ministry of women in their role of assistance has been vital to the gospel endeavor. Such a role is not to be considered as less important than preaching and teaching. David reminded his two hundred warriors not to think that they had a more exalted position than those who had stayed behind with the baggage. "For as his share is who goes down to the battle, so shall his share be he who stays by the baggage: they shall share alike" (1 Sam 30:24). They struggled together, though they did it in different roles, and they shared together

---

[84] Derek, 119.

[85] Arndt and Gingrich, 791; BDAG, 964.

in the reward. Such also is the shared labor and reward of men and women in the gospel, although they perform their ministries in different roles.

Priscilla

In connection with his gospel work in Corinth, Paul met one of the most fascinating couples in the Bible and maintained friendship and fellowship with them the rest of his life.

> After these things he left Athens and went to Corinth. And he found a Jew named Aquila, a native of Pontus, having recently come from Italy with his wife Priscilla, because Claudius had commanded all the Jews to leave Rome. He came to them, and because he was of the same trade, he stayed with them and they were working, for by trade they were tent-makers.
> (Acts 18:1-3).

It is possible that Paul introduced this couple to Christianity, but it is more probable that they had already been believers in Rome, and their dispersion had something to do with that fact.[86] They later accompanied Paul to Ephesus, where they extended greetings to their old friends in Paul's first letter to the Corinthians (Acts 18:18-19; 1 Cor 16:19). Evidently, they made their way back to Rome, for Paul greets them in that letter as his "fellow workers" (Rom 16:3). However, this much traveled couple evidently left that imperial city again, for Paul greets them in his last letter, written from Rome (2 Tim 4:19). Wherever they went, this "missionary couple" sought to win

---

[86] F.F. Bruce, *The Book of Acts* (Grand Rapids: Wm. B. Eerdmans Publishing Co., 1970), 368-69.

the lost and provide a place for believers to worship. They were one of many families (and women) who had "a church in their house" (Rom 16:5; Cf. also Nympha: Col 4:15).

It is in connection with their stay at Ephesus that they engaged in work of particular interest. When Apollos, an eloquent Alexandrian who was knowledgeable in the Scriptures, came to Ephesus and powerfully preached the facts of Jesus' life as they fulfilled Old Testament scriptures. "But when Priscilla and Aquila heard him, they took him aside and explained to him the way of God more accurately" (Acts 18:26). Notice of this action is taken by a prominent Evangelical Feminist.

> Priscilla and Aquila apparently had a marvelously emancipated marriage, since both of them were tent-makers (Acts 18:3) and both of them were teachers of the Word (Romans 16:3). More than one excellent scholar believes that Priscilla may even have been the author of the Epistle to the Hebrews.[87]

This comment neglects two obvious facts: (1) they did this instruction together as a team; and (2) they did this instruction to Apollos privately. There is nothing in this passage to indicate that Priscilla was a "teacher of the Word" in the formal sense. Furthermore, they are not called "teachers of the Word" in Romans 16:3 but are called "fellow workers." In much the same way a modern missionary could refer to one of the couples on his field as "fellow-workers," without implying that the wife's role was the same as the husband's.

That Priscilla authored the book of Hebrews was first proposed by Adolph Harnack and held by James H. Harris, Arthur Peaks and James Moulton, and has occasionally been

---

[87] Mollenkott, 17-18.

revived.[88] Although the theory is worthy of serious consideration, it rests on some basic assumptions that can be seriously questioned: (1) that the letter was written to believers in Ephesus; (2) that Priscilla was Peter's convert in Rome, according to 2:3; (3) that Hebrews reflects Philo's influence, and that Priscilla knew Philo in Rome; (4) that Priscilla was a traveling companion of Timothy (13:23); and (5) that Priscilla deliberately used a masculine participle in 11:32 (*diegoumenon* - διηγούμενον) to conceal her femininity. Every theory for the authorship of Hebrews rests on some assumptions, and the matter should well be left, at best, as "an educated guess."

As has been noted before, the case of Priscilla serves as another warning to not read into a text more than it says. Such "assumptive exegesis" is characteristic of much of the writing regarding women's place in the ordained ministry.

Women in Rome

The sixteenth chapter of the Epistle to the Romans should be particularly noted by those who malign Paul as a misogynist. Although the gender of one name is in question, out of the twenty-nine people addressed, at least nine are women.

Phoebe

The first woman mentioned in Romans 16:1 was a very prominent one, although she was not a resident of Rome. She was from Cenchrea, a port of the larger city of Corinth and probably the bearer of this epistle to its destination.

> I commend to you our sister Phoebe, who is a
> servant (*diakonon* - διάκονον) of the church
> which is at Cenchrea; that you receive her in

---

[88] Ruth Hoppin, Priscilla: *Author of the Epistle to the Hebrews* (New York: Exposition Press, 1969).

the Lord in a manner worthy of the saints, and
that you help her in whatever matter she may
have need of you; for she herself has also been
a helper (*prostatis* - προστάτις) of many, and also
of myself (Rom 16:1-2).

The significance of Phoebe for those who desire a
greater prominence for women in the church cannot be
minimized. Dr. Virginia Mollenkott on this very point declares
as follows.

Romans 16:1-2 refers to Phoebe as both
diakonos and *prostatis*. The latter word
means "one who presides," –a president,
ruler, patron, superintendent or manager.
Why have translators obscured the force of
this word by translating it merely as
"succorer" (KJV) or "helper" (RSV)? Paul
uses the word *diakonos* twenty-one times,
and in the King James Version eighteen of
those times the word is translated
"minister" and three times as "deacon."
But the only time Paul applies the word to
a woman, the translators see fit to translate
the word as "servant"! Thus we have been
denied the knowledge that Phoebe was a
minister or deacon of the church at
Cenchrae, and that she was designated as a
"ruler over many" by the apostle Paul.[89]

Because of the crucial question of the meaning of these
terms applied to Phoebe, some closer attention must be paid

---

[89] Mollenkott, 18. See also Scanzoni and Hardesty, 62; Spencer, 219-
220; and Russell C. Prohl, *Women in the Church* (Grand Rapids: Wm.
B. Eerdmans Publishing Co., 1957) 70ff. See Westfall, 271-72.

to them to discern their precise meanings. The noun *prostatis* (προστάτις), translated as "succorer" (KJV) or "helper" (NASB), is a *hapax legomenon*, or a word that appears only in this passage in the New Testament. Since there is no other Scriptural reference to the word, its occurrences outside the New Testament are crucial. In Classical Greek the word was used with only one definition: "protectress." The masculine form *prostates* (προστάτης), however, was used in three ways: (1) "chief, ruler, leader;" (2) "protector, patron, guardian," and (3) "suppliant."[90] Therefore, when the above writers affirm the meaning of *prostatis* as "one who presides, etc.," they are referring to only one meaning of a similar yet different word in classical Greek. Furthermore, as the word moved from classical into Koine Greek, it came to mean "protectress, patroness, helper." The acknowledged authority in NT Greek lexicons cites the following writers that use the word in this sense: Cornutus (1st century A. D.), Lucian (2nd century A. D.), Cassius Dio (2nd-3rd century A. D.), and papyri from the same time as Paul. Furthermore, the masculine form *prostates* dropped altogether its meaning of "one who presides" and came to mean "defender, guardian."[91] There is no reference in Koine Greek that has been found in which *prostatis* ever means "one who presides, president, leader, etc." Yet one modern writer states, "In Koine Greek the word (*prostatis*) means 'one who presides; the chief of a party; a president, ruler, foreman, superintendent'."[92] Paul Jewett, who himself believes strongly

---

[90] See Liddell-Scott-Jones for its use as the equivalent of the Latin word for "patron" or in this case "matron" (1526). See Montonari's *Brill Dictionary of Ancient Greek* for the translation of the feminine word προστάτις as "protectress, patroness" (1827).

[91] Bauer, Arndt, Gingrich, 726; BDAG, 885.

[92] Spencer, 219-220. Spencer does not cite any primary source but simply gives as her source "Russell C. Prohl, *Women in the Church*, 70." Prohl, however, refers not to *prostatis* (προστάτις), but to

in the right of women to ordination, admits that this word has been wrongly used.

> In this passage, προστάτις should hardly be taken to mean that Phoebe was a woman "ruler." Rather the meaning would seem to be that she was one who cared for the affairs of others by aiding them with her resources. [93]

Further evidence that *prostatis* in this verse does not mean "president" or some similar idea is found in the verse itself. After Paul commends Phoebe to the believers at Rome he asks that they might receive her and help her in whatever needs she has. The reason why they should do this is because she has been a *prostatis* "of many, and of myself as well." Is Paul saying that Phoebe had been his "president, ruler, chief"? How much better sense is it if Paul says that Phoebe has been a "patroness" of the church and also of me, in accordance with the use of the word in Koine Greek.[94] Under what

---

prostates (προστάτης), a different word with a meaning in classical Greek that *prostatis* does not have in NT Greek, "ruler" (GE, 1827).

[93] Jewett, 170n. Ryrie's treatment of this passage suffers due to his lack of the knowledge supplied by the lexicons. He is forced to "explain away" the word, which he thinks means "president." Charles Ryrie, *The Role of Women in the Church* (Chicago: Moody Press, 1970), 87-89.

[94] The translation "she was designated as a ruler over many by me," suggested by Scanzoni and Hardesty, 62, is simply without any warrant from the Greek text. It would require the translation of "designate" for *ginomai* (γίνομαι), which it never means (cf. Arndt and Gingrich, 157-59; BDAG, 196-99). Such a translation also totally disregards the following phrase "also of me." Phoebe was not Paul's president but she was his benefactor.

circumstances she was a helper of the church we do not know. She may have been a woman of some wealth and helped the church materially, or a woman of prominence who protected the church in a civil way. The help she offered Paul may have been the kind offered by Lydia (Acts 16:15). The other word that describes Phoebe in Romans 16:1 is *diakonon* (διάχονον), the accusative form of *diakonos* (διάχονος), translated as "servant" in the KJV and NASB. Since this word raises the issue of the diaconate in the early church, we will postpone our treatment of it until the next section.

> In any case Phoebe is one of the women memorialized in the New Testament by their devoted service to the gospel whose honor is not to be tarnished by elevation to positions and functions inconsistent with the station they occupy in the economy of human relationships.[95]

The first couple in this chapter is the familiar Priscilla and Aquila. Note the different spelling of her name, Prisca, and that she was mentioned before her husband.

> Greet Prisca and Aquila, my fellow workers in Christ Jesus, who for my life risked their own necks, to whom not only do I give thanks, but also all the churches of the Gentiles; also *greet* the church that is in their house (Rom 16:3-5).

Since we have already discussed this gifted half of an important husband-wife team, we will pass on to the other women in the chapter. Mary is greeted in verse 6 as one "who

---

[95] John Murray, *The Epistle to the Romans* (Grand Rapids: Wm. B. Eerdmans Publishing Co., 1965), II, 227.

has worked hard (*ekopiasen* - ἐκοπίασεν) for you." Tryphaena, Tryphosa and Persis are noted that they "worked hard" (same verb) in the Lord (v. 12). Rufus' mother is greeted, and Paul refers to her as a mother to him also (v. 13). He probably does not mean this literally, but refers with affection to one who no doubt cared for him in a special way. Finally, he greets Julia and Nereus' sister (v.15). It is evident from this listing that women in Rome labored hard in the furtherance and maintenance of gospel work. The exact nature of their labor, however, cannot be determined with any certainty.

The second clearly mentioned couple appears in 16:7 and we will give special attention to the female partner, Junia. The NASB, however, reads her name as masculine: "Greet Andronicus and Junias, my kinsmen and my fellow prisoners, who are outstanding among the apostles, who also were in Christ before me" (Rom 16:7). In doing so, the NASB departs from a tradition that began with Tyndale and the KJV and continues down to the translations used by evangelicals which uniformly translate the name as the feminine, Junia (e.g., NKJV, NET, ESV, CSB, and NIV11; only the New Jerusalem Bible agrees with the NASB masculine translation). It seems best to acknowledge that this person was a woman and the way the pair is mentioned is consistent with the use of Prisca and Aquila in verse 3 as a husband-wife team.[96]

More controversial is how best to translate the prepositional phrase *epistemoi en tois apostolois* (ἐπίσημοι ἐν τοῖς ἀποστόλοις). Does it convey the idea "outstanding among the apostles" (KJV, NKJV, NASB, NIV) or the idea "outstanding" or "notable to the apostles" (ESV, NET, CSB)? The author does not desire to burden the reader with a technical discussion

---

[96] Textual critic Eldon Epps has brought forth evidence that the feminine spelling with a different accent may have been suppressed in some circles (Eldon Jay Epp, *Junia: The First Woman Apostle*, (Minneapolis: Fortress, 2005). The evidence clearly supports the feminine identity of this name-bearer (see note in the NET Bible).

of the use of the dative case as either locative or instrumental, which obviously has good scholars on each side. For the sake of argument, I will assume that the expression describes both Andronicus and Junia as being "among the apostles."[97] But what does it mean IF Junia is described as an "apostle"? We should not forget that some individuals in the NT are called by that title who would never be included among the "Twelve" or who would bear the same authority as they did along with Paul (Barnabas, Titus, and Epaphroditus, e.g., as well as the itinerant "apostles" described in the first century *Didache*). Even egalitarians often acknowledge that she was what we call today a "missionary."[98] It is highly doubtful that she was an apostle in the same sense as Paul and the Twelve (see the distinction between the "twelve" and the "apostles" in 1 Cor 15:5-7). Junia's ministry in a patriarchal world was probably with other women, for a wife had access to women's areas which would not be generally accessible to a man. Andronicus and Junia comprised a "peripatetic pair" who served the Christian cause much like Priscilla and Aquila. This is another example of how some egalitarians simply conclude more than is necessary from a Biblical reference. An "apostle" in the early church was one who witnessed Jesus' ministry and resurrection (Acts 1) but was not necessarily an "elder" or an "overseer." We should rightfully applaud the efforts of these dedicated women, but we should not conclude from their sacrificial witness that they were what we today call "pastors" who were ordained to authoritatively "rule" and "teach" local congregations.

Deaconesses

The other word that describes Phoebe in Romans 16:1

---

[97] For an excellent article defending the translation "by the apostles" see M.H. Burer and D.B. Wallace, "Was Junia Really an Apostle? A Re-examination of Rom 16.7," *NTS* 47 (2001):76 – 91.

[98] Payne, 66.

is *diakonon* (διάκονον), the accusative of *diakonos* (διάκονος), translated as "servant" in the KJV and NASB. This appellation has raised the question of whether or not Phoebe is the first example of an order of "deaconesses" that eventually developed in the post-apostolic church. If so, it would be the only time in the New Testament that the word is clearly applied to a woman. The question is highly debated and centers around whether or not *diakonos* should be taken in a general or official sense. The word appears 30 times in the New Testament, and is translated 20 times as "minister," 7 times as "servant," and 3 times as "deacon." The translation "minister" does not carry the same idea as the way that term is used in the current century, i.e., the ordained pastor of a church. The idea, rather, is "one who ministers," or "servant." The word differs, however, from the more common word for "servant" (*doulos* - δοῦλος). The *diakonos* is a servant in relation to his work, while a *doulos* is a servant in relation to a person, hence the translation "slave."[99]

There are at least 3 other occurrences of *diakonos* in the official sense of "deacon," an officer in a local church. In his letter to the Philippians Paul sends his greetings to all the saints "along with the overseers ("bishops" – [*episkopois* - ἐπισκόποις]) and deacons (*diakonos* - διακόνοις)" (Phil 1:1). It is important to note that deacons are linked with bishops and mentioned after them. No other mention, however, is made of their

---

[99] Richard Chevenix Trench, *Synonyms of the New Testament* (London: James Clarke and Co., LTD., 1961), 30-31. Kittel mentions the following uses of *diakonos* (διάκονος) as "servant" in the New Testament: (1) "waiter at a meal," John 2:5, 9; (2) "servant of a master" Mt. 22:13; (3) "servant of a spiritual power" 2 Cor. 11:14; (4) "servant of Christ" 2 Cor. 11:23; (5) "servant of God" I Th 3:1-3; (6) "heathen authorities" Rom. 13:1-4; and (7) "servant of the church" I Cor. 3:5. Herman Beyer, διάκονος in *Theological Dictionary of the NT*, ed. Gerhard Kittel, trans. Geoffrey Bromiley (Grand Rapids: Wm. B. Eerdmans Publishing Co., 1964), II, 88-89. See also BDAG, 230-31.

qualifications or duties in the epistle.

The diaconate stands in a close relationship with the episcopate in later epistles. In 1 Timothy 3:1-7 qualifications are listed for a bishop and this is followed by a list of requirements for a deacon.

> Deacons likewise must be men of dignity, not double-tongued, or addicted to much wine or fond of sordid gain, but holding to the mystery of the faith with a clear conscience. These men must also first be tested; then let them serve as deacons if they are beyond reproach... Deacons must be husbands of only one wife, and good managers of their children and their own households. For those who have served well as deacons obtain for themselves a high standing and great confidence in the faith that is in Christ Jesus (1 Tim 3:8-10, 12-13).

These requirements refer to males, since one of the requirements is that the deacon be a "one-wife husband" (v.12). The question that is highly debated centers on the following verse: "Women must likewise be dignified, not malicious gossips, but temperate, faithful in all things" (1 Tim 3:11). The word translated "women" in the NASB and "wives" in the KJV is the plural of *gune* (γυνή), which can mean either "woman" or "wife," according to the contexts.[100] It has not been uncommon in the history of interpretation to translate this word as "women," thus taking the verse as referring to deaconesses."[101] If these commentators are correct, it should be remembered that the diaconate is not a

---

[100] Arndt and Gingrich, 167; BDAG, 209.

[101] Ryrie, 90.

preaching/teaching ministry in the New Testament. As we examine the characteristic attributes of the overseer and deacon in 1Timothy 3:1-13, we must conclude that the requirements in character for each office are similar. However, there is one characteristic required for the overseer that is not required of the deacon. "An overseer, then, must be ... able to teach" (1 Tim 3:12). So even if a female diaconate can be demonstrated, it does not mean that this diaconate consists of a preaching/teaching ministry,

However, from the evidence that we have in the NT it is doubtful if such a diaconate existed. If *gunaikas* (γυναῖκας) means "women" in verse 11, then it interrupts the whole train of thought in the passage, because Paul returns to the male deacon's requirements in verse 12 when he says, "Let deacons be husbands of only one wife... ." Paul's concern is the consistency of a husband and wife in their spiritual and familial responsibilities. That wives of deacons may have aided their husbands in their responsibilities is a most definite probability.

Applying this information about the use *diakonos* to its use of Phoebe in Romans 16:1, it is highly doubtful that it is used for her in any official way. Finally, does not the masculine gender of *diakonos* lend support to the idea of its general use in its reference to Phoebe? If there was an official office of deaconess, why was there not an official word – something say, like *diakone* (διάκονη)? Also, doesn't the absence of the article with *diakonos* speak of its general use in this verse? Phoebe is not "the pastor" of the church, but was "a servant" of the church. Although these arguments are not conclusive in themselves, they do support the interpretation that Phoebe is spoken of as one who has rendered great service to the assembly at Cenchreae, but is not to be considered as one of its elders or official leaders. Perhaps the use of *diakonos* conveys the sense of a "courier" or bearer of a letter, the way it is used in Col 1:7 and other places. Phoebe was thus a *prostatis* (προστάτις) in the sense of a "patroness." She was a *diakonos* (διάκονος) in the sense of a "ministering servant" or "courier."

Conclusion on Women as Elders/Overseers

Articulate and impassioned appeals for the full ordination of women in church ministry have appeared regularly in recent years. In this regard, notice should be given to the bibliography of related works since 1976, the original date of this thesis. More and more male ministers and scholars are affirming this egalitarian position.[102]

That women exercised an active ministry in the New Testament has been obvious from the foregoing. Further aspects of that ministry are developed in the next chapter. However, to view such women as Lydia, Euodias, Syntyche, Priscilla, and Phoebe as maintaining an authoritative teaching/preaching ministry to men, as elders/overseers, is to read more into the texts than they actually say. Some egalitarian advocates have admitted that the traditional texts that we have treated above appear to limit the authoritative teaching and ruling roles to men (see e.g., the recent works by McKnight and Bird). At the same time they stress examples in the NT of women ministering and conclude that the texts that limit women's ministry should be interpreted in light of the texts that mention their ministry, thus concluding that all levels of ministry should be open to women. I firmly suggest that the examples of women ministering should be interpreted in the light of programmatic texts like 1 Timothy 2 and 1 Corinthians 14. Whatever Priscilla, Phoebe, Junia, Euodias and Syntyche were doing, it was within the framework of Paul's commands. This is the real hermeneutical issue at hand. Descriptive texts should be interpreted in the light of prescriptive texts, not vice versa. This is a sound hermeneutical principle that is utilized often in the study of events and practices in the Book of Acts, just to mention one example. When we do that we can discern better exactly what these ministering women were doing and

---

[102] See, e.g., Alan Johnson, ed. *How I Changed my Mind About Women in Leadership: Compelling Stories From Prominent Evangelicals* (Grand Rapids: Zondervan, 2010).

we do not end up pitting scripture against scripture.

These ministering women of the NT, set free by Christ and sometimes lifted out from the burdensome social restrictions of a post-Biblical Judaism, ministered freely and joyfully. However, their ministry roles did not contradict the guidelines based on the dynamic of creation, fall, and redemption. These guidelines are clearly expressed in the programmatic texts of 1 Corinthians and the Pastoral Epistles.

WHAT THEN SHOULD WE DO?

After an examination of the Scriptural commands, prohibitions, and examples cited in the previous chapters, it is the settled conviction of this writer that the teaching/ruling function of the church (the "elder/bishop") should be limited to males by Divine design. The reason for this restriction is grounded not in any time-bound cultural situation, but in the permanently valid order of creation and fall. A real and fruitful function of women in the ministry of the church has already been evident from examples cited of certain women who labored in the New Testament Church in various ministries. It is the purpose of this chapter to more fully explore the opportunities of ministry open to women in connection with the church.

Mother

Although it is not directly related to the ministry of the church, the role of a woman as a mother is vitally important to the church. Scripture abounds in statements of a vastly important molding influence that a mother has on her child (Prov 1:8; 6:20; 31:15, 27-31). Many women do not fully realize the contribution that they can make to the work of Christ by properly training, guiding, and instructing their children. Consider the following passages.

> For I am mindful of the sincere faith within you, which first dwelt in your grandmother Lois, and your mother Eunice, and I am sure that it is in you as well (2 Tim 1:5).

> You, however, continue in the things you have learned and become

> convinced of, knowing from whom
> you have learned *them*, and that from
> childhood you have known the sacred
> writings which are able to give you the
> wisdom that leads to salvation through
> faith which is in Christ Jesus (2 Tim
> 3:14-15).

What a contribution a godly mother and grandmother made to the world and the church when they invested their lives in a growing child named Timothy! One of the requirements of a widow to be "enrolled" by a church is that "she has brought up children" (1 Tim 5:10). The word "brought up" is the Greek word *eteknotrophesen* (ἐτεκνοτρόφησεν) and is closely related to the word in the command to fathers about their children: "bring them up (*ektrephete* - ἐκτρέφετε) in the discipline and instruction of the Lord" (Eph 6:4). To bring up a child does not just relate to their physical well-being, but to every area of their growth – spiritual, emotional, etc. An alternate interpretation of the difficult clause, "women will be preserved through the bearing of children" (1 Tim 2:15) may refer to this ministry. After his strong prohibition of women's teaching men in 2:12-14, he may be saying that a woman's greatest contribution is in another sphere, i.e. in the bearing, rearing and teaching of her children. It is through that ministry that she will be preserved as she exhibits a godly example before them.

Why do some women despise this obligation and privilege and opt for a career with their children in someone else's care? Certain unexpected hardships and circumstances, such as widowhood or disability of her husband may necessitate such a decision. But the choice of a mother to simply further her career at the expense of her children can only indicate a spirit of rebellion against God's order for her. Some women need to realize the tremendous effect on society they can have by their ministry in the home. It may not be as dramatic as a so-called "career," nor may the results be seen as quickly, but the lasting results will be far more permanent. "Women can make a tremendous contribution to the world from the bottom up instead of from the top down."[103]

What about women to whom God has not granted the blessing of children? Or what of those whose children have departed from home? There is still much that they can do in this regard. One of the most profitable ministries can be that of an "adopted aunt" or "adopted grandmother" to some child in the church. This child may not have a mother or may be from a large family of children. This is often appropriate, especially when the child may not have natural grandparents or other relations nearby. Such a ministry can confirm and supplement the parental instruction delivered at home. Although such a ministry can be profitable through teaching in Sunday School, it needs to be recognized that a personal ministry can be even more effective.[104]

Teaching

Another similar area of ministry recognized in the New Testament is that of the older women to the younger women.

> Older women likewise are to be reverent in their behavior, not malicious gossips nor enslaved to much wine, teaching what is good, so that they may encourage (*sophronizosin* - σωφρονίζωσιν) the young women to love their husbands, to love their children, *to be* sensible, pure, workers at home, kind, being subject to their own

---

[103] Wayne Mack, *The Role of Women in the Church* (Cherry Hill, NJ: Mack Publishing Co., 1972), 68.

[104] The author and his wife can personally testify how such "grandparents" and their single daughter served us and our children during the ministry in our first church.

husbands, so that the word of God will not
be dishonored (Tit 2:3-5).

The teaching by word and example of an experienced woman
can be of great encouragement to those who desire to learn
how they can be better wives and mothers. Some of those
ministries can be performed much better by women than men.
Women may open up to other women about personal
problems which would be improper to discuss with men. It is
important that godly, experienced women engage in this
counseling and teaching lest some younger women begin to
share their problems and gossip with others who cannot really
help them. Such a ministry does not need to be limited to
"older women" teaching "younger women," but the important
matter is that those women who are knowledgeable in the
Word and experience share that knowledge with those women
who need it.

Is there ever a situation when women are permitted to
teach men? Some egalitarians love to bring up the examples of
female missionaries in other countries who have helped to
found churches. Were they wrong? First of all, we are usually
talking about exceptional cases when these examples are cited.
They are not the norm. Second, let me clearly affirm that I do
not judge ladies in isolated ministry situations where they have
to take the lead because there were no males to do so.
Although I cannot cite examples in the NT, I would rather a
pagan or a new convert without access to a male preacher
receive instruction from a woman rather than be denied the
truth. There are many examples in the history of missions
where such women are eager to see male leadership take over
what they have started because there were no men to do it.
Perhaps, therefore, we should not create a situation where a
single woman has to make that choice. I believe, therefore, that
women serving as part of a team ministry, not as isolated
singles, can contribute much to the Gospel cause working with
male leadership.

The question of women teachers of theology in college

and seminaries is another challenge as to how we should apply this restriction. There are some first rate evangelical women scholars today, and since colleges and seminaries are not churches, how should these restrictions apply to them? One needs to ask if such Bible and theology professors should be considered as elder-qualified to function in these roles. If such professors are to be elder-qualified, then the answer is that the NT restrictions apply to these professors as well. That is the policy of such institutions as The Master's University and Seminary, and it seems eminently reasonable and right.

Widows

In the early church "widows" performed an important function that needs to be recovered today. The Old Testament often espouses the cause of the widow and orphan in their plight. God is spoken of as "a judge for the widows" (Psa 68:5) and the law pronounced, "Cursed is he who distorts the justice due to an alien, orphan, and widow" (Deut 27:19). The regulations of the marriage of a widow by her brother-in-law after the death of her husband helped to protect the rights of the widow. Such a situation was not required, however (Deut 25:5-10). Therefore, many widows were forced to live alone and become objects of charity (Deut 24:19; Ruth 2). In the intertestamental period their cause was taken up by the temple authorities, and a fund was established for them (2 Maccabees 3:10).

After Pentecost some of the widows became members of the first Christian community. The new believers naturally assumed responsibility for them. Some felt that the distribution was not being done properly, and a real dispute was created over the matter. The dispute resulted in further organization of the church (Acts 6:1-7).

By the time that the Pastoral Epistles were written, the Apostle Paul evidently thought that the whole matter needed regulating and issued the following guidelines to protect against abuse.

Honor widows who are widows indeed; but if any widow has children or grandchildren, they must first learn to practice piety in regard to their own family and to make some return to their parents; for this is acceptable in the sight of God. Now she who is a widow indeed and who has been left alone, has fixed her hope on God and continues in entreaties and prayers night and day. But she who gives herself to wanton pleasure is dead even while she lives. Prescribe these things as well, so that they may be above reproach. But if anyone does not provide for his own, and especially for those of his household, he has denied the faith and is worse than an unbeliever. A widow is to be put on the list only if she is not less than sixty years old, *having been* the wife of one man, having a reputation for good works; *and* if she has brought up children, if she has shown hospitality to strangers, if she has washed the saints' feet, if she has assisted those in distress, *and* if she has devoted herself to every good work. But refuse *to put* younger widows *on the list*, for when they feel sensual desires in disregard of Christ, they want to get married, *thus* incurring condemnation, because they have set aside their previous pledge. At the same time they also learn *to be* idle, as they go around from house to house; and not merely idle, but also gossips and busybodies, talking about things not proper *to mention*. Therefore, I want younger *widows* to get married, bear children, keep house, *and* give the enemy no occasion for reproach; for some have already turned aside to follow Satan. If any woman who is a believer has *dependent* widows, she must assist them and the church must not be burdened, so that it may assist those who are widows indeed (1 Tim 5:3-16).

Although the passage has sometimes been taken as supporting some sort of "order of widows" that ministered for the church, the following principles evident in the passage seem to rule that out. (1) Relatives must assume the support of widows whenever possible (vv. 4, 8, 16). (2) The church must support those who are unable to be supported by relatives. These are called "widows indeed" (vv. 3, 5, 9, 16). (3) These enrolled widows did have a ministry of prayer for the church, but nothing is stated about additional responsibilities (v. 5). (4) Relief by the church was certainly not limited to enrolled widows, though it was assumed in the cases of all enrolled widows. (5) Younger women are advised to marry, and no preference was given to celibacy (vv. 11-15). (6) The work of women is still primarily connected with the home. "Therefore, I want the younger widows to get married, bear children, keep house, and give the enemy no occasion for reproach" (v. 14).[105]

The modern attempt by the federal government to assist various unfortunate groups has caused the church to retreat from its responsibility in this regard. Such "benefits" can often be a help, especially when they have been earned by years of labor on the part of the husband. However, churches should never allow their own to become dependent on the state for their existence. To do so is to abnegate their spiritual and temporal responsibilities.

I have personal knowledge of a widow in our ministry who lost her husband to cancer. She has become the living

---

[105] Ryrie, 81-85.

embodiment of what Paul taught about ministering widows in the above passage.

Music

Although a public ministry of the Word is forbidden to women in mixed assemblies, there is evidence and example from Scripture that they may participate fully in the church in other ways. Scriptural evidence has been cited previously regarding the participation of women in singing and instrumental ministries of the temple in the Old Testament. Although the elaborate temple ritual was not found in the persecuted "home-churches" of the early church, there is certainly no reason to forbid women from singing in choirs and playing instruments when such is possible today (Eph 5:19). Songs and music are to be rendered to the Lord and do not involve any exercise of authority over others.

Prayer

Previous attention has also been given to passages which speak of women praying in the assemblies (1 Tim 2:8; 1 Cor 11:5). Anna also prayed in the temple and gave thanks to God (Luke 2:36-38). From these examples there seems to be little basis for the practice of not permitting women to pray audibly in mixed meetings. It should be remembered that prayer is to be directed to God and does not involve the exercise of authority over others. The public giving of thanks to God should be encouraged, and all should participate – men and women.

Testimony

Previous notice has been given of the witness to others by women who had been touched physically and spiritually by Jesus (e.g. John 4:28-42). Jesus did not discourage such bearing of testimony. The public giving of "testimonies" to what God has done in a life should be encouraged, both by males and females. Testimonies do not involve the exercise of authority – they combine praise of God with encouragement to others. Some writers believe that the charismatic gift of prophecy in these days is served by what may be called the "testimony."

> Nor is prophecy an exercise of authority, for it is not premeditated authoritative teaching, but the sharing of thought, praise or testimony at the impulse of the Spirit in a way spiritually beneficial to those present. Prophecy builds us up spiritually, but it is not the exposition of the Scriptures. Perhaps prophecy would include speaking praise of God, testifying to how He saved one or helped in one's Christian life, speaking a word of comfort or a word of encouragement to the believers.[106]

Any woman giving testimony should be careful not to "preach" to those who hear her. However, any man giving a testimony should also be careful not to "preach," for that is not the purpose of a testimony.

Hospitality

One of the requirements of a widow to be enlisted exemplifies another way in which women can profitably serve in church related ministries. She is to be one who "has shown hospitality to strangers...." (1 Tim 5:10). Hospitality is a good work that is incumbent on all believers, and particularly for elders' families (Heb 13:1-2; Matt 25:35; Rom 12:1; 1 Pet 4:9;

---

[106] Leroy Birney, *The Role of Women in the New Testament Church* (Middlesex: Christian Brethren Research Fellowship Publications, 1971), 16-18.

1Tim 3:2). In the history of the early church such women as Mary, Lydia, Phoebe, and Nympha (better reading) exhibited hospitality in allowing their homes to be used for meetings of believers (Acts 12:12; Acts 16:15; 1 Cor. 16:19; Col. 4:15). John commended believers in his epistles for receiving itinerant workers and caring for them (2, 3 John). Too often homes of believers are shut off to the brethren and those who miss the blessing are the ones behind the doors. Such activities as home Bible studies, prayer cells, lodging missionaries and itinerants, or just being a place where lonely people can find help and encouragement can make a home a real vital ministry in a church.

Relieving the Afflicted

Another characteristic of an enlisted widow is that "she has washed the saints' feet," and that "she has assisted those in distress...." (1 Tim 5:10). Her concerns do not focus solely on her house and children, but on others. "Washing the feet" is a menial task, no doubt despised by many, yet very needful in those days. It exhibits a servant's attitude, which was the attitude of Jesus (John 13:1-20). This may mean literally washing the saints' feet, if the saints' feet need to be washed. However, it refers also to the menial tasks done to help relieve others. Dorcas didn't preach, but she "washed the saints' feet" by making clothes for the widows who needed them (Acts 9:36-42). A ministry to the afflicted whether in body or soul, can be one of the most rewarding activities in which a woman can engage. "Until there are no afflicted or burdened people in the world, women have plenty to do for Christ."[107]

These few activities mentioned certainly do not exhaust the many ways in which women can serve Christ today. The creative woman, under the leadership of God's Spirit, will never find her lot in life dull, uninteresting, and lacking in challenge. That she is not allowed the ministry of teaching and

---

[107] Mack, 75.

ruling men does not imply her inferiority; it affirms that an orderly God desires His order to be visually represented before His people. There are many women whose abilities exceed that of men. The issue, however, is not one of ability but of function. The Christian woman who has learned the secret of submitting her will to God, which is required of every believer, will find no problem in submitting to her God-ordained sphere of ministry. Not only will she do that, but she will thank Him for the privilege of serving Him in any way.

Conclusion

I fully realize that my approach to women's ministry is out of step with current religious teaching, even among many if not most evangelicals. But hear me out in this my final plea.

The church has often been charged with lagging behind the rest of the world. For the church to "take a cue" from the society is not necessarily evil – if that "cue" is consistent with Scriptural responsibilities that the church has neglected. However, if the church simply desires to follow a movement to "keep up with the times," and that movement has definite unscriptural emphases, then the church is guilty of "worldliness" in the true sense of the word. In this writer's opinion, the overall thrust of "Evangelical Feminism" is a bit "worldly" in this sense.

I write these strong words knowing that there are some sincere evangelical scholars among those calling for an egalitarian approach to women's ordination as elder/overseers. I fully recognize the contemporary role of evangelical women in Biblical scholarship, especially those who currently teach in colleges and seminaries. Having interacted closely with their arguments, however, I come away with a sense that their explaining the appropriate Biblical texts often results rather in explaining them away. In my opinion, this explaining away the evident meaning of these texts is necessary in order to justify women's ordination as elders and overseers.

The church should constantly be examining her doctrines and methods in the light of the Word. That which is contrary to the Word must be abandoned or adjusted. But if the church bows to prevailing pressures without any clear Scriptural warrant, even if it is from well-meaning evangelicals, the long term results will be negative.

True freedom is not experienced by seeking the right to do what we want; it is attained by submission to the One who gives us the power to do what we ought. May Christian men and women everywhere seek to be faithful "bondslaves" of the One who in bondage to Him in reality sets us free.

Bibliography to 1976

Books

Arndt, William F., and Gingrich, F. Wilbur. *Greek-Engligh Lexicon of the New Testament and other Early Christian Literature.* Chicago:University of Chicago Press, 1957.

The Babylonian Talmud. Translated and edited by Rabbi Dr. I. Epstein. London: The Soncino Press, 1948, 35 volumes.

Barnes, Albert. *Notes on Thessal onians, Timothy, Titus and Philemon.* Grand Rapids; Baker Book Hausa, 1969.

Birney, Leroy. *The Role of Women in the New Testament Church.* Middlesex, England: Christian Brethren Research Fellowship, 1971.

Bonar, Andrew. *Exposition of Leviticus.* Grand Rapids: National Foundation for Christian Education, 1970.

Bruce, E. F. *The Book of Acts.* Grand Rapids: Wm. B. Eerdmans Publishing Co., 1970.

_____. *The Letters of Paul.* Grand Rapids: Wm. B. Eerdmans Publishing Co., 1965.

Bruce, Michael, and Duffield, G.E. (eds.) *Why Not? Priesthood and the Ministry of Women.* London: Marchem Books, 1972.

Chantry, Walter J. *Signs of the Apostles.* Edinburgh: Banner of Truth Trust, 1973.

Church of Scotland. *The Place of Women in the Church.* Edinburgh: St. Andrews Press, 1959.

Classic Greek Dictionary. Chicago: Follatt Publishing Go., 1956.

Cohen, A. *Everyman's Talmud.* New York: E. P. Button and Co., 1949

Dabney, Robert. *Discussions: Evangelical and Theological.* London: Banner of Truth Trust, 1967.

Danielou, Jean. *Ministry of Women in the Early Church.* London: Faith Press, Ltd., 1961.

deBeauvoir, Simone. *The Second Sex.* Translated and edited by H. M. Parshley, New York: Bantam Books, 1961.

Fitzwater, P. B. Woman. *Her Mission, Position and Ministry.* Grand Rapids: Wm. B. Eerdman's Publishing Co., 1969.

Guthrie, Donald. *The Pastoral Epistles.* London: Tyndale Press, 1957.

Hendriksen, William. *Exposition of the Pastoral Epistles*. Grand
    Rapids: Wm. B. Eerdman's Publishing Co,, 1957.
Hodge, Charles. *Systematic Theology*. Grand Rapids: Wm. B.
    Eerdmn's Publishing Co., 1970.
Hoppin, Ruth. *Priscilla:Author of the Epistle to the Hebrews*. New York:
    Exposition Press, 1969.
Jeremias, Joachim. *Jerusalem in the Time of Jesus*. Philadelphia:
    Fortress Press, 1969.
Jewett, Paul. *Man as Male and Female*. Grand Rapids: Wm. B.
    Eerdman's Publishing Co., 1975.
Josephus, Flavius. *Antiquities of the Jews*. Translated by H. St. J.
    Thackeray, in The Loeb Classical Library. Edited by E. H.
    Warmington. London: William Heineman, Ltd., 1967.
Knight; George W. III. *The Role Relation of Men and Woman and the
    Teaching/Ruling Functions in the Church*. St. Louis, 1975.
Knowling, R. J. "Acts of the Apostles" in *Expositor's Greek
    Testament*. Grand Rapids: Eerdman's Publishing Co., 1951.
Lenski, R.C.H. *Paul's First and Second Epistles to the Corinthians*.
    Minneapolis: Augsburg Publishing House, 1963.
Lockman Foundation. *New American Standard Bible*. Carol Stream,
    IL: Creation House, 1971; 1995.
Mack, Wayne. *The Role of Women in the Church*. Cherry Hill, N.J.:
    Mack Publishing Co., 1972.
Moule, C.F.D. *The Phenomenon of the New Testament*. London: SCM
    Press, Ltd.. 1967.
Murray, John. *The Epistle to the Romans*. Grand Rapids: Wm. B.
    Eerdmans Publishing Co., 1955.
Neil, James. *Everyday Life in the Holy Land*. London: Cassell and
    Company, Ltd., 1913.
Olthuis, James. *I Pledge You My Troth*. New York: Harper and Row
    Publishers, 1975.
Philo. *In Flaccum*. Translated by F. H. Colson, in The Loeb Classical
    Library. Ed T. E. Page. London: William Heineman, Ltd.
    1929.
Prohl, Russell. *Woman in the Church*. Grand Rapids: Wm. B.
    Eerdman's Publishing Co., 1957.
Quebedeaux. Richard. *The Young Evangelicals*. New York: Harper
    and Row Publishers, 1974.
Reuther, Rosemary, (ed.). *Religion and Sexism*. New York: Simon and
    Schuster. 1974.

Robertson A.T. and Plummer, A. *1 Corinthians*. Edinburgh: T. and T. Clark, 1914.

Robertson, A. T. *Grammar of the Greek NT in the Light of Historical Research*. New York: Hodder and Stoughton, 1914.

Ryrie, Charles. *The Role of Women in the Church*. Chicago: Moody Press. 1970.

Sayers, Dorothy. *Are Women Human?* Grand Rapids: Wm. B. Eerdman's Publishing Co., 1971.

Scanzoni, Letha and Hardesty, Nancy. *All We're Meant To Be*. Waco, Texas: Word Books, Inc., 1974. 3rd revised edition 1992.

Schechter, Solomon. *Studies in Judaism*. Philadelphia: Jewish Publication Society of America, 1896.

Smith, J.B. *Greek-English Concordance*. Scottdale, Pa.: Herald Press, 1955.

Stendahl, Krister. *The Bible and the Role of Women: Case Study in Hermeneutics*. Philadelphia: Fortress Press, 1966.

Strauss, Lehman. *Speaking in Tongues*. Philadelphia: Bible Study Time, 1979.

Kittel, Gerhard, (ed.). *Theological Dictionary of the New Testament*. Translated by Geoffrey Bromiley. Grand Rapids: Wm. B. Eerdman's Publishing Co., 1964.

Thrall, Margaret. *The Ordination of Women to the Priesthood*. London: SCM Press Ltd., 1958.

Trench, Richard C. *Synonyms of the New Testament*. London: James Clarke and Co., Ltd., 1961.

Warfield, Benjamin B. *Counterfeit Miracles*. London: Banner of Truth Trust, 1972.

West, Nathaniel. *Women and Church Ministry*. Alden, N.Y.: Star Route, Box 11, n.d.

Wheeler, Richard S. *Pagans in the Pulpit*. New Rochelle, N.Y. Arlington House, 1974.

Vos, Clarence. *Woman in Old Testament Worship*. Delft, The Netherlands: N.V. Judels and Brinkman, 1968.

Zerbst, Fritz. *The Office of Women in the Church*. Translated by Albert Markens. St. Louis: Concordia Publishing House, 1955.

Articles and Periodicals

Beale, Alex. "Petticoats in the Pulpit." *Crusade*, March 1975, 19-20.
_____. "Seen but not heard." *Crusade*, April 1975, 19-20.

Beyer, Herman. "διάκονος" in *Theological Dictionary of the New Testament*, ed. Gerhard Kittel, trans. Geoffrey Bromiley. Grand Rapids: Wm. B. Eerdman's Publishing Co., 1969, II, 31-93.

Boldrey, Dick and Joyce. "Women in Paul's Life." *Trinity Studies*, II (1972), 1-36.

Carson, Herbert. "Women in the Church." *Reformation Today*, Spring, 1971, 4-10.

Cooper, John. "St. Paul's Evaluation of Women and Marriage." *Lutheran Quarterly*, Vol. 16 (1964), 291-302.

Dayton, Donald. "An Egalitarian View." *Post American*, May 1975. 3-15.

_____, and Lucille Sider. "Recovering a Heritage: Evangelical Feminism." *Post American*, September, 1974, 7-9.

_____. "Women as Preachers: Evangelicals Precedents." *Christianity Today*, May 23, 1975, 4-6.

Derek, Thomas. "The Place of Women in the Church at Philippi." *The Expository Times*, Vol. 84, No. 4 (January, 1972), 117-120.

Elliott, Elisabeth. "Why I Oppose the Ordination of Women." *Christianity Today*. June 6, 1975, 12-16.

Foh, Susan. "The Women Question." *The Presbyterian Guardian*, Vol. 45, No. 2 (February, 1976), 2-7.

Ford, Joseph Massyngberde. "Biblical Material Relevant to the Ordination of Women." *Journal of Ecumenical Studies*, 10 (Fall, 1973), 669-694.

Hardesty, Nancy. "Women: Second Class Citizens?" *Eternity*, January, 1971, 14-16, 24-29.

Hilder, G. F. "Women and the Ministry." *Theology*, 57 (December, 1954), 452-456.

Howard, Thomas. "A Dialogue on Women, Hierarchy, and Equality." *Post American*, May, 1975, 8-15.

Hurley, James B. "Did Paul Require Veils or the Silence of Women?" *Westminster Theological Journal*, Vol. XXXV, No. 2 (1973) 190-220.

Jewett, Paul King. "Why I Favor the Ordination of Women." *Christianity Today*, June 6, 1975, 7-12.

Lewis, C.S. "Priestesses in the Church," in *God in the Dock* (Grand Rapids: Wm. B. Eerdman's Publishing Co., 1970), 234-239.

Martin, William J. "I Corinthians 11:2-16: An Interpretation." in

Apostolic History and the Gospel. Edited by W. Ward Gasque and Ralph P. Martin. (Grand Rapids: Wm. B. Eerdman's Publishing Co., 231-241.

Mcleod, Donald. "The Place of Women in the Church." *Banner of Truth*, No. 81 (June, 1970), 31-40.

Mascall, E.L. "The Ministry of Women." *Theology* 57 (Nov. 1954), 428-429.

Mollenkott, Virginia. "Church Women, Theologians, and the Burden of Proof." *Reformed Journal*, (July-August, 1975), 18-30; (September, 1975),

Narkis, Bezalel. "Women." *Encyclopedia Judaica*, Vol. 16.

Neal, Marshall. "Women at Work and Worship." *Faith for the Family*, March/April 1974, 41-42.

Oepke, Albrecht. " γύνη" in *Theological Dictionary of the New Testament*, ed. Gerhard Kittel, trans. Geoffrey Bromiley. (Grand Rapids: Eerdmans, 1964), I, 1976-1989.

Robbins, Irene. "St. Paul and the Ministry of Women." *Expository Times*, XLIV (January, 1935), 185-188.

Reumann, John. "What in Scripture Speaks to the Ordination of Women. *Concordia Monthly*, 44 (January, 1973) 1-30.

Scaer, David. "What Did St. Paul Want?" *His*, May, 1973, 11-14, 18.

Scanzoni, Letha. "Feminists and the Bible." *Christianity Today*, February 2, 1973, 10-15.

_____. "Woman's Place: Silence or Service?" *Eternity*, February, 1966, 14-16.

Spencer, Aida Dina Besancon. "Eve at Ephesus." *Journal of the Evangelical Theological Society*, Vol. 17, No. 4 (Fall, 1974),

Swidler, Leonard. "Jesus was a Feminist." *Catholic World*, January, 1971, 177-183.

Thrall, Margaret. "The Ordination of 'Women to the Priesthood." *Theology*, 57 (September, 1954), 330-335.

Trible, Phyllis. "Depatriarchalizing in Biblical Interpretation." *Journal of the American Academy of Religion*, 12 (March, 1973), 30-48.

Weeks, Noel. "Of Silence and Head Covering." *Westminster Theological Journal*, XXV (Fall, 1972), 21-27.

Bibliography Since 1976

My thanks to Paul Felix and Indira Usmanova for their assistance with this bibliography. I have attached an asterisk (*) to books and articles which basically support the complementarian position that I have defended in this book, although there are a few asterisks about which I may need correction!

Allen, Ronald and Beverly Allen. *Liberated Traditionalism: Men and Women in Balance.* A Critical Concern Book. Portland, Ore.: Multnomah, 1985.*

Allison, Robert W. "Let Women be Silent in the Churches (1 Cor. 14:33b-36): What did Paul Really Say, and What Did It Mean?" *JSNT* 32 (1988): 27-60.

Archer, G. L. "Does 1 Timothy 2:12 Forbid the Ordination of Women?" *Encyclopedia of Bible Difficulties.* Grand Rapids: Zondervan, 1982.*

Ashcroft, Mary Ellen. *Balancing Act: How Women Can Lose Their Roles and Find Their Callings.* Downers Grove, Ill.: InterVarsity Press, 1996.

Bacchiocchi, Samuele. *Women in the Church: A Biblical Study on the Role of Women in the Church.* Berrien Springs, Mich.: Biblical Perspectives, 1987.*

Barnett, Paul W. "Wives and Women's Ministry (I Timothy 2:11-15)." *Evangelical Quarterly* 61, 3 (1989): 225–38. Reprinted in *Evangelical Review of Theology* 15 (4, 1991): 321–34.

Barron, Bruce. "Putting Women in their Place: 1 Timothy 2 and Evangelical Views of Women in Church Leadership." *Journal of the Evangelical Theological Society* 33 (1990): 451-59.

Baugh, S. M. "The Apostle Among the Amazons," *Westminster Theological Journal* 56 (1994): 153-71.*

_____. "Feminism at Ephesus: 1 Timothy 2:12 in Historical Context." *Outlook* 42 (May, 1992): 7–10.*

Beck, James R., and Craig L. Blomberg. *Two Views on Women in Ministry*. Counterpoints. Edited by Stanley N. Gundry. Grand Rapids: Zondervan, 2001.

Belleville, Linda L. "Ἰουνιαν ἐπίσημοι ἐν τοῖς ἀποστόλοις: A Re-examination of Romans 16.7 in Light of Primary Source Materials." *NTS* 51 (2005): 231-49.

_____. *Women Leaders and the Church: Three Crucial Questions*. Grand Rapids: Baker, 2000.

Bilezikian, Gilbert G. *Beyond Sex Roles: What the Bible Says about A Woman's Place in Church and Family*. Grand Rapids: Baker, 1985 (2nd ed. 1987).

Bird, Michael. *Bourgeois Babes, Bossy Wives, and Bobby Haircuts: A Case for Gender Equality in Ministry*. Grand Rapids: Zondervan, 2014.

Blakenhorn, David, Don Browning, and Mary Stewart Van Leeuwen. eds. *Does Christianity Teach Male Headship?*. Grand Rapids: Eerdmans, 2004.

Bloesch, Donald G. *Is the Bible Sexist? Beyond Feminism and Patriarchalism*. Westchester: Crossway, 1982.*

Blomberg, Craig L. and Thomas Schreiner "Women in Ministry: A Complementarian Perspective." James Beck, ed. *Two Views on Women in Ministry*. Grand Rapids: Zondervan, 2005.*

Boldrey, Richard, and Joyce Boldrey. *Chauvinist or Feminist? Paul's View of Women*. Grand Rapids: Baker, 1976 (formerly published as "Women in Paul's Life." *Trinity Studies* 2 [1972]: 1-36).

Boomsma, Clarence. *Male and Female, One in Christ: New Testament Teaching on Women in Office*. Baker, 1993.

Borland, James A. "Women in the Life and Teachings of Jesus." Pages 113–23 in *Recovering Biblical Manhood and Womanhood: A Response to Evangelical Feminism*. Ed by J. Piper and W. Grudem. Wheaton, Illinois: Crossway, 1991.*

Bowman, Ann L. "Woman in Ministry: An Exegetical Study of 1 Timothy 2:11-15." *Bibliotheca Sacra* 149 (1992): 193 – 213. *

Bruce, F.F. "One in Christ Jesus: Thoughts on Galatians 3:26-29." *Journal of the CBRF* 122 (1990): 7 – 10.

Burer, Michael H., and Daniel B. Wallace. "Was Junia Really an Apostle? A Re-examination of Rom 16.7." *NTS* 47 (2001):76 – 91.*

Burton, Keith A. "1 Corinthians 11 and 14: How Does a Woman Prophesy and Keep Silence." *Journal of the Adventist Theological Society* 10 (1999): 268–84.

_____. "Women, Teaching, Authority, Silence: 1 Tim 2:8–15 and 1 Pet 3:1-6." *Journal of the Adventist Theological Society* 10 (1999): 285–90.*

Carson, D.A. "'Silent in the Churches': On the Role of Women in 1 Corinthians 14:33b-36." Pages140-53 in *Recovering Biblical Manhood and Womanhood: A Response to Evangelical Feminism.* Eds. Piper and Grudem. Wheaton: Crossway, 1991.*

Cerling, Charles Edward, Jr. "Women Ministries in the New Testament Church." *JETS* 19 (1976): 209 – 15.

Clark, Gordon. "The Ordination of Women." *Trinity Review* 17 (January, 1981): 1-6.*

Clark, Stephen B. *Man and Woman in Christ: An Examination of the Roles of Men and Women in Light of Scripture and the Social Sciences.* Ann Arbor, Mich.: Servant, 1980.

Clouse, B., and R.G. Clouse, eds. *Women in Ministry: Four Views.* With contributions from R.D. Culver, S. Foh, W. Liefeld, and A. Mickelsen. Downers Grove, Ill.: InterVarsity Press, 1989.

Cohick, Lynn. *Women in the World of the Earliest Christians.* Baker, 2009.

Conn, Harvie. "Evangelical Feminism: Some Bibliographical Reflections on the Contemporary State of the 'Union.'" *WTJ* (1984): 104 – 24.*

Cooper, John W. *A Cause for Division? Women in Office and the Unity of the Church*. Grand Rapids: Calvin Seminary, 1991.*

Council on Biblical Manhood and Womanhood, The. *The Danvers Statement*. Wheaton, Ill: The Council on Biblical Manhood and Womanhood, 1988.*

Culver, Robert D. "A Traditional View: Let Your Women Keep Silence." Pages 25–52 in Bonnidell, Clouse, and Robert G. Clouse, eds. *Women in Ministry: Four Views*. Downers Grove, Ill: InterVarsity Press, 1989.*

Davies, G. and John Woodhouse. "The Ordination of Women: Are the Arguments Biblical?" *Southern Cross* (July, 1985): 17-18.*

Doriani, Daniel. *Women and Ministry: What the Bible Teaches*. Wheaton: Crossway, 2003.*

Duncan, J. Ligon, and Susan Hunt. *Women's Ministry in the Local Church*. Wheaton: Crossway, 2006.*

Edwards, Ruth B. *The Case for Women's Ministry*. London: SPCK, 1989.

Eldred, O. John. *Women Pastors: If God Calls, Why Not the Church?* Valley Forge: Judson, 1981.

Elliott, John H. "Jesus Was Not an Egalitarian: A Critique of an Anachronistic and Idealist Theory." *Biblical Theology Bulletin* 32 (2002): 75-91.*

Ellis, E. Earle. "Paul and His Co-Workers." *NTS* 17 (1970 – 71): 437 – 52.

Epp, Eldon Jay. *Junia: The First Woman Apostle*. Minneapolis: Fortress, 2005.

Eunjoo, Mary Kim. *Women Preaching: Theology and Practice through the Ages*. Cleveland: The Pilgrim Press, 2004.

Fee, Gordon. "The Cultural Context of Ephesians 5:18 – 6:9." *Priscilla Papers* 16.1 (2002): 3-8.

_____. "Woman in Ministry: The Meaning of 1 Timothy 2:8 – 15 in Light of the Purpose of 1 Timothy." *Journal of the Christian Brethren Research Fellowship* (Wellington, NZ] 122 (1990): 11 – 18.

Felix, Sr., Paul W. "The Hermeneutics of Evangelical Feminism." Pages 373–405 in *Evangelical Hermeneutics: The New Versus the Old.* Edited by R.L. Thomas. Grand Rapids: Kregel, 2002.*

Fiorenza, Elizabeth Schüssler and Hermann Häring, eds. *The Non-Ordination of Women and the Politics of Power.* Maryknoll, N.Y.: Orbis Books, 1999.

_____. and Mary Collins. *Women: Invisible in Church and Theology.* Edinburgh, UK: T. and T. Clark Limited, 1985.

Fish, John H. III. "Women Speaking in the Church: The Relationship of 1 Corinthians 11:5 and 14:34-36." *The Emmaus Journal* 1, no. 3 (1992): 214-251.*

Fitzmyer, J.A. "Another Look at ΚΕΦΑΛΗ in 1 Corinthians 11.3." *NTS* 35 (1989): 503 – 11.

_____. "*Kephalē* in I Corinthians 11:3" *Int* 47.1 (1993): 52 – 59.

Foh, Susan T. *Women and the Word of God: A Response to Biblical Feminism.* Philadelphia: Presbyterian and Reformed, 1979.*

France, R. T. *Women in the Church's Ministry: A Text Case for Biblical Hermeneutics.* Didsbury Lectures, 1995. Exeter: Paternoster, 1995.

Gangel, Kenneth O. "Biblical Feminism and Church Leadership." *Bibliotheca Sacra* 140 (1983): 55-63.*

Gasque, W. Ward. "Role of Women in the Church, in Society, and in the Home." *Crux* 19.3 (1983): 3-9.

Grenz, Stanley J. "Anticipating God's New Community: Theological Foundations for Women in Ministry." *JETS* 38 (1995): 595 – 611.

Grenz, Stanley J. with Denise Muir Kjesbo. *Women in the Church: A Biblical Theology of Women in Ministry.* Downers Grove, Ill., InterVarsity Press, 1995.

Gritz, Sharon Hodgin. *Paul, Women Teachers, and the Mother Goddess at Ephesus: A Study of 1 Timothy 2:9-15 in Light of the Religious and Cultural Milieu of the First Century.* Lanham, New York, and London: University Press of America, 1991.

Groothuis, Rebecca Merrill, *Good News for Women: A Biblical Picture of Gender Equality.* Grand Rapids, Baker, 1996.

Grudem, Wayne. *Biblical Foundations for Manhood and Womanhood.* Wheaton, Ill.: Crossway, 2002.*

_____. *Evangelical Feminism and Biblical Truth.* Wheaton, Ill.: Crossway, 2012.*

_____. "The Meaning of κεφαλή ('Head'): An Evaluation of New Evidence, Real and Alleged." *JETS* 44 (2001): 25-65.*

_____. "Prophecy – Yes, But Teaching – No: Paul's Consistent Advocacy of Women's Participation without Governing Authority." *JETS* 30 (1987): 11 – 23.*

Hassey, Janette. *No Time for Silence: Evangelical Women in Public Ministry Around the Turn of the Century.* Grand Rapids: Zondervan Academie Books, 1986.

House, H. Wayne. *The Role of Women in Ministry Today.* Nashville: Thomas Nelson, 1990. Rev ed, Grand Rapids: Baker, 1995.*

Hove, Richard. "Does Galatians 3:28 Negate Gender-Specific Roles?" *Biblical Foundations for Manhood and Womanhood,* ed. W. Grudem, 105-153. Wheaton: Crossway Books, 2002).*

_____. *Equality in Christ? Galatians 3:28 and Gender Dispute.* Wheaton: Crossway Books, 1999).*

Huber, Randal. *Called, Equipped and No Place to Go: Women Pastors and the Church.* Anderson, Ind.: Warner Press, 2003.

Irwin, D. "The Ministry of Women in the Early Church: Archaeological Evidence." *Duke Divinity Review* 45 (1980): 76-86.

Jewett, Paul K. *The Ordination of Women: An Essay on the Office of Christian Ministry.* Grand Rapids: Wm. B. Eerdmans, 1980.

Johnson, Alan, ed. *How I Changed my Mind About Women in Leadership: Compelling Stories From Prominent Evangelicals.* Grand Rapids: Zondervan, 2010.

Hurley, James B. *Man and Woman in Biblical Perspective.* Leicester: Inter-Varsity Press, 1981; Grand Rapids: Zondervan, 1981.*

Keener, Craig S. *Paul, Woman and Wives: Marriage and Women's Ministry in the Letters of Paul.* Peabody, Mass.: Hendrickson, 1992.

Kloha, Jeffrey John. *A Textual Commentary on Paul's First Epistle to the Corinthians.* PhD thesis, University of Leeds, 2006. Available online: http://etheses.whiterose.ac.uk/296/.*

Köstenberger, Andreas J. and Thomas R. Schreiner, eds. *Women in the Church: An Analysis and Application of 1 Timothy 2:9 – 15.* 2nd ed. Grand Rapids: Baker, 2005.*

Knight III, George W. *The Role Relationship of Men and Women: New Testament Teaching.* Chicago: Moody Press, 1977; rev., 1985.*

Kroeger, Catherine Clark. *A Quick Reference Guide to I. Biblical Records of Women in the Early Church; II. Jesus, the Friend of Women; III. Old Testament Considerations Regarding Women.* St. Paul, Minn.: Christians for Biblical Equality, 1995.

Kroeger, Catherine Clark and Mary Evans, eds. *The InterVarsity Press Women's Bible Commentary.* Downers Grove, Ill.: InterVarsity Press, 2002.

Kuhns, Dennis R. *Women in the Church.* Scottsdale Herald Press, 1978.

La Porte, Jean. *The Role of Women in Early Christianity, Studies in Women and Religion,* 7. Lewiston, N.Y.: Edwin Mellen, 1982.

Lee-Barnewall, Michelle. *Neither Complementarian nor Egalitarian: A Kingdom Corrective to the Evangelical Gender Debate.* Baker, 2016.

Leonard, Juanita Evans, ed. *Called to Minister: Empowered to Serve: Women in Ministry.* Anderson, Ind.: Warner Press, 1989.

Litfin, Duane. "Evangelical Feminism—Why Traditionalists Reject It." *Bibliotheca Sacra* 136 (1979): 258-71.*

Luter, A. Boyd, "Partnership in the Gospel: The Role of Women in the Church at Philippi." *JETS* 39 (1996): 411 – 20.

MacArthur, John. *God's High Calling for Women.* Chicago: Moody Press, 2009.*

May, Melanie A., ed. *Women and Church.* Grand Rapids: Eerdmans, 1991.

McKnight, Scot. *Junia Is Not Alone.* Englewood: Patheos Press, 2011.

Mickelsen, Alvera, ed. *Women, Authority and the Bible.* Downers Grove, Ill.: InterVarsity Press, 1986.

Mickelsen, Berkley, and Alvera Mickelsen. *Women and the Bible.* Downers Grove, Ill.: InterVarsity Press, 1985.

Mollenkott, Virginia. *Women, Men, and the Bible.* Crossroad Publishing Co. 1989 (rev ed).

_____ . *Omni-Gender: A Trans-Religious Approach.* Pilgrim Press, 2007 (expanded edition).

Montonari, Franco. *Brill Dictionary of Ancient Greek* Leiden, Boston: Brill, 2015 (GE).

Moo, Douglas J. "1 Timothy 2:11 – 15: Meaning and significance." *TJ* 1 NS (1980): 62 – 83.*

Newsom, Carol A. and Sharon H. Ringe, eds. *Women's Bible Commentary.* Louisville: Westminster John Knox. 1998.

Osborne, Grant R. "Hermeneutics and Women in the Church." *JETS* 20 (1977): 337 – 52.

Osburn, Carroll, ed. *Essays on Women in Earliest Christianity.* 2 vols. Joplin, Missouri: College Press, 1993, 1995.

_____. *Women in the Church: Refocusing the Discussion.* Abilene, Texas: Restoration Perspectives, 1994.

Osiek, Carolyn. *A Woman's Place: House Churches in Earliest Christianity.* Minneapolis: Fortress Press, 2005.

Pape, Dorothy R. *God and Women: A Fresh Look at What the New Testament Says about Women.* Downers Grove, Ill.: InterVarsity Press, 1975 and Oxford: Mowbrays, 1978.

Patterson, Dorothy and Rhonda Kelley, eds. *The Woman's Study Bible.* Nashville: Thomas Nelson, 1995.*

Payne, Philip B. "1 Tim 2.12 and the Use of οὐδε to Combine Two Elements to Express a Single Idea." *New Testament Studies* 54, 2 (2008): 235-53.

_____. "Distigmai Matching the Original Ink of Codex Vaticanus: Do They Mark the Location of Textual Variants? Pages 191-213 in Patrick Andrist, ed., *Le manuscrit B de la Bible* (Vaticanus gr. 1209): Introduction au fac-similé, Actes du Colloque de Genève, contributions supplémentaires. Prahins, Switzerland: Éditions du Zèbre, 2009.

_____. "Examining the Twelve Biblical Pillars of Hierarchy." *Priscilla Papers* Special Edition for ETS (Autumn 2012).

_____. "Fuldensis, Sigla for Variants in Vaticanus, and 1 Cor 14.34-5." *New Testament Studies* 41 (1995): 240-62.

_____. "Galatians 3:28's Application of Paul's New Creation Teaching to the Status of Women in Christ." Priscilla Papers Special Edition Journal for ETS (Autumn 2012).

_____. *Man and Woman, One in Christ: An Exegetical and Theological Study of Paul's Letters.* Grand Rapids: Zondervan, 2009.

_____. "Ms. 88 as Evidence for a Text Without 1 Cor 14.34-5." *New Testament Studies* 44 (1998): 152-58.

_____. "The Text-Critical Function of the Umlauts in Vaticanus, with Special Attention to 1Corinthians 14.34-35: A Response to J. Edward Miller" *Journal for the Study of the New Testament* 27, 1 (2004): 105-12.

_____. "What Does Kephalē Mean in the New Testament? Response." Pages 118-32 in *Women, Authority & the Bible.* Edited by Alvera Mickelsen. Downers Grove: InterVarsity Press, 1986.

Pierce, Ronald W., and Rebecca Merrill Groothuis. *Discovering Biblical Equality: Complementarity without Hierarchy.* Downers Grove, Ill.: InterVarsity Press, 2004.

Piper, John, and Wayne Grudem, eds. *Recovering Biblical Manhood and Womanhood: A Response to Evangelical Feminism.* Wheaton, Illinois: Crossway, 1991.*

Porter, Stanley E. "What Does it Mean to be 'Saved by Childbirth' (1 Timothy 2.15)?" *Journal for the Study of the New Testament* 49 (1993): 87-102.*

Poythress, V.S. "The Church as Family: Why Male Leadership in the Family Requires Male Leadership in the Church." Pages 233-47 in *Recovering Biblical Manhood and Womanhood: A Response to Evangelical Feminism.* Eds Piper and Grudem. Wheaton: Crossway, 1991.*

Richardson, Peter. "From Apostles to Virgins: Rom 16 and Roles of Women in the Early Church." *TJT* 2.2 (1986): 232 – 61.

Saucy, Robert L. "Women's Prohibition to Teach Men: An Instigation into Its Meaning and Contemporary Application." *JETS* 37 (1994): 79 – 97.*

Saucy, Robert L. and Judith Ten Elshof, *Women and Men in Ministry: A Complementary Perspective.* Chicago: Moody Press, 2001.*

Scholer, David. *Women in Early Christianity.* Studies in Early Christianity 14. New York: Garland Publishing, 1993.

Schreiner, Thomas R. "An Interpretation of 1 Timothy 2:9-15: A Dialogue with Scholarship." Pages 85-120 in *Women in the Church: An Analysis of 1 Timothy 2:9-15*. Köstenberger and Schreiner, eds. 2nd ed. Grand Rapids: Baker, 2005.*

_____. "A Review of Philip Payne: Man and Woman in Christ" in the *Journal of Biblical Manhood and Womanhood*. Spring, 2010. Volume XV, Number One: 33-46.*

_____. "Women in Ministry: Another Complementarian Perspective." *Two Views on Women in Ministry*. Ed. James Beck. 2nd ed. Grand Rapids: Zondervan, 2005.*

Shack, Jennifer. "A Text Without 1 Corinthians 14.34-35? Not According to the Manuscript Evidence." *Journal of Greco-Roman Christianity and Judaism*, 10 (2014) 90-112.*

Spencer, Aída Dina Besançon. *Beyond the Curse: Women Called to Ministry*. Nashville: Nelson, 1985.

Strauch, Alexander. *Biblical Eldership*. Littleton, Co.: Lewis and Roth Publishers, 1995.*

_____. *Men and Women: Equal Yet Different: A Brief Study on the Biblical Passages on Gender*. Littleton, Co.: Lewis and Roth Publishers, 1999.*

Swidler, Leonard. *Biblical Affirmations of Woman*. Philadelphia, Westminster, 1979.

_____. *Women in the Ministry of the New Testament*. Paulist, 1980.

Thorley, John. "Junia, a Woman Apostle." *NovT* 38 (1996): 18 – 29.

Torjesen, Karen Jo. *When Women Were Priests: Women's Leadership in the Early Church and the Scandal of Their Subordination in the Rise of Christianity*. San Francisco: HarperCollins, 1993.

Tucker, Ruth A., and Walter Liefeld. *Daughters of the Church: Women and Ministry from New Testament Times to the Present*. Grand Rapids: Zondervan, 1987.

Waltke, Bruce K. "The Role of Women in the Bible." *Crux* 31.1 (1995): 29 - 40.

Ware, Bruce. "Equal in Essence, Distinct in Roles: Eternal Functional Authority and Submission among the Essentially Equal Divine Persons of the Godhead." *Journal for Biblical Manhood and Womanhood* 13, no. 2 (2008): 43-58.*

Webb, William J. *Slaves, Women and Homosexuals: Exploring the Hermeneutics of Cultural Analysis.* Downers Grove, Ill: InterVarsity Press, 2001.

Westfall, Cynthia Long. *Paul and Gender: Reclaiming the Apostle's Vision for Men and Women in Christ.* Grand Rapids: Baker, 2016.

Williams, Don. *Paul and Women in the Church.* Ventura: Regal, 1977.*

Witherington, Ben, III. *Women and the Genesis of Christianity.* Edited by Ann Witherington, Cambridge: Cambridge Press, 1990.

_____. *Women in the Earliest Churches.* SNTSMS 59. Cambridge: Cambridge Univ. Press, 1988.

Westfall and Payne offer some of the best scholarly arguments for an egalitarian view of Paul's theology and practice.

Knight, Grudem and Schreiner offer some of the best scholarly arguments for a complementarian view of women's ministry.

ABOUT THE AUTHOR

William Varner is Professor of Biblical Studies at The Master's University in Santa Clarita, California. He also is Pastor of the Sojourners Fellowship at Grace Community Church in Sun Valley, California.